Alzheimer's Disease

A FORGOTTEN LIFE

Elaine Landau

Franklin Watts®

A Division of Scholastic Inc.
New York • Toronto • London • Auckland • Sydney
Mexico City • New Delhi • Hong Kong
Danbury, Connecticut

Alzheimer's Disease: A Forgotten Life

Photographs © 2005: Alzheimer's Disease Education & Referral Center: 39; Corbis Images: 6 (Bettmann), 93 (Unger Kevin/Sygma), 11, 17 (Tom Stewart); Envision Stock Photography Inc./ Photononstop: 55, 64; Feldman H. Gracon: 45; Getty Images: 81 (Alex Freund/Stone), 5, 19 (Photodisc Collection), cover (Jeremy Rendell/Taxi); J.N. Browndyke: 27, 33, 95; Photo Researchers, NY: 91, 97 (Simon Fraser/MRC Unit, Newcastle General Hospital/SPL), 57 (Will & Deni McIntyre), 16 (National Library of Medicine/SPL); PhotoEdit: 87 (Tony Freeman), 71, 88 (Frank Siteman), 24 (Merritt Vincent), 67 (David Young-Wolf); photolibrary.com/Picture Plain: 47, 79; Phototake/Pr. JJ Hauw: 32; PictureQuest/Image Source: 52; The Image Works: 31, 37 (Richard Lord), 43 (Dion Ogust), 12 (Rhoda Sidney), 76 (Nita Winter); Visuals Unlimited/Ralph Hutchings: 40.

Cover design by Marie O'Neill
Book design by The Design Lab

Library of Congress Cataloging-in-Publication Data
Landau, Elaine.
 Alzheimer's disease : a forgotten life / by Elaine Landau.
   p. cm.
 Includes bibliographical references and index.
 ISBN 0-531-16755-0
 1. Alzheimer's disease. I. Title.
 RC523.L363 2005
 616.8'31—dc22   2005001736

Contents

Introduction 5

CHAPTER ONE
Alzheimer's Disease 11

CHAPTER TWO
All About Alzheimer's Disease. 31

CHAPTER THREE
Treatment 55

CHAPTER FOUR
Caring for Someone with
        Alzheimer's Disease 71

CHAPTER FIVE
The Future 91

Source Notes. 103
Glossary. 106
To Find Out More. 108
Index 109

Alzheimer's Disease: A Forgotten Life

Introduction

The sad news filled the nation's airwaves and sent the country into mourning. Former President Ronald Reagan was dead at the age of ninety-three. He died on June 5, 2004, as a result of **Alzheimer's disease (AD)**. While his death was a tremendous loss to his family, those close to the Reagans claimed that in some ways he had actually been gone for a long time.

Signs that something was wrong had begun quite a while before. Once, during a regularly scheduled checkup with his White House physician, President Reagan had jokingly said, "I have three things that I wanted to tell you today. The first is that I seem to be having a little problem with my memory. I cannot remember the other two."[1] The joke was made well before any serious symptoms had surfaced, and it had been too early to diagnose the problem. Yet, joking aside, it's possible that President Reagan knew that something was wrong. Often people in the early stages of Alzheimer's disease sense a growing loss of their mental capabilities.

The situation worsened as time passed. Near his eighty-third birthday Reagan spoke in Washington, D.C., before

Ronald Reagan was a former actor and an excellent public speaker.

2,500 people. Although no one would have imagined it that day, it would be the last speech he ever gave. Reagan was equipped with his notes, and the presentation had gone well enough. It wasn't until the former president and Nancy, his wife of more than forty years, returned to their hotel suite that things began to unravel. Suddenly President Reagan paused and, turning to his wife, said, "Well, I have got to wait a minute. I am not quite sure where I am." [2]

This was not an isolated incident. On other recent occasions, the former president had seemed somewhat confused and forgetful. At times, even simple tasks had begun to be cumbersome. Realizing that they might be facing a serious medical problem, Mrs. Reagan took her husband for a consultation at the Mayo Clinic in Rochester, Minnesota. There they learned that it was likely that Ronald Reagan was suffering from Alzheimer's disease.

The diagnosis would become increasingly clear to Nancy Reagan in the months and years ahead. While some days her husband seemed perfectly normal, at other times he didn't remember that he'd ever been president or lived in the White House. Wanting to say goodbye to the American public and realizing that this was something he could not afford to put off, President Reagan handwrote an open letter to all of America (see next page).

The deterioration caused by Alzheimer's disease was made public in the former president's case. Most people with AD, however, never experience a nation's sympathy. They deal with this debilitating illness privately. Those stricken, along with their families, soon learn that AD is an incurable progressive brain disorder that takes a terrible toll on people's lives. It robs them of the ability to remember, to learn, and to make sound judgments.

As the disease progresses, they experience difficulty communicating, keeping a job, and meeting even their most basic needs. With the passage of time, patients frequently experience personality changes, often becoming anxious, suspicious, or upset much of the time. This can make things especially difficult, as they frequently come to mistrust the people trying to care for them. Some become delusional as well. At times, Alzheimer's disease may seem like a devastatingly slow way to die. That was why Nancy Reagan referred to it as a long goodbye.

A DAUGHTER'S VIEW

"In some ways we were lucky. My father never had episodes of violent frustration, although it's understandable that many people do. Memories are being incinerated, turned to ash and dust. There is no cure, no medicine to vanquish the vanquisher. Alzheimer's always wins in the end."

Patti Davis (President Ronald Reagan's daughter) Newsweek, June 21, 2004

My Fellow Americans:

I have recently been told that I am one of the millions of Americans who will be affected by Alzheimer's disease. Upon learning this news, Nancy and I had to decide whether as private citizens we would keep this a private matter or we would make this news known in a public way. In the past Nancy had suffered from breast cancer and I had my cancer surgeries. We found that through our open disclosures we were able to raise public awareness. We were happy that as a result many more people underwent testing. They were treated in the early stages and were able to return to normal healthy lives. So now we feel it is important to share it with you.

In opening our hearts, we hope that this might promote greater awareness of the condition. Perhaps it will encourage a clearer understanding of the individuals who are affected by it. At the moment, I feel just fine. I intend to live the remainder of the years God gives me on this Earth, doing the things I have always done. I will continue to share life's journey with my beloved Nancy and family. I plan to enjoy the great outdoors and stay in touch with my friends and supporters.

Unfortunately, as Alzheimer's disease progresses, the family often bears a heavy burden. I only wish there was some way I could spare Nancy from this painful experience. When my time comes, I am confident that with your help she will face it with faith and courage.

In closing let me thank you, the American people, for giving me the great honor of allowing me to serve as your president. When the Lord calls me home, whenever that may be, I will leave with the greatest love for this country of ours and eternal optimism for its future. I now begin the journey that will lead me into the sunset of my life. I know that for America, there will always be a bright dawn ahead.

Thank you, my friends. May God always bless you.

Sincerely,
Ronald Reagan[3]

A NATIONAL PROBLEM

The problem of Alzheimer's disease is far more widespread than most people think. It's been half-jokingly said that if something isn't done about Alzheimer's disease soon, there will only be two types of elderly people in the future—those with Alzheimer's disease and those caring for them.

This is because people are living longer as a result of current medical advances, as well as because a large generation of baby boomers (people born after World War II) is reaching an advanced age. It's estimated that one in nine baby boomers could live to be one hundred while only one out of five hundred in their grandparents' generation did so. As more people live into their eighties and nineties, a larger number of individuals will fall victim to the diseases of aging—including Alzheimer's disease.

While Alzheimer's disease comes at a tremendous personal cost to those facing it, there are also substantial financial costs involved. The national yearly cost of caring for people with Alzheimer's disease may be as high as $100 billion.[4] As more people within an aging population fall victim to this disorder, the costs to the country are expected to skyrocket. Alzheimer's disease affects not only individual families but society as a whole. In one way or another, it is a problem that will eventually touch the lives of all Americans.

This is a book about the various facets of Alzheimer's disease. It explores the causes, diagnostic tools, and treatments available today. It also discusses the research that may lead to some important advances in the fight against this devastating affliction. The medical aspects of Alzheimer's disease are further explored by Dr. Jeffrey Browndyke in the Ask Dr. Browndyke sections within each chapter. Dr. Browndyke is an assistant professor in the Department of Psychiatry and Behavioral Sciences at Duke University

Medical Center in Durham, North Carolina, and is a faculty member of the Joseph and Kathleen Bryan Alzheimer's Disease Research Center at Duke.

Because Alzheimer's is a disease that affects the whole family, the role of the caregiver is discussed as is the toll this illness can take on the affected person's loved ones. Throughout the book you'll hear both the stories and the voices of people with Alzheimer's and those closest to them. All the people in the book are real—their feelings and responses are as genuine as the ongoing research that holds out hope for a brighter tomorrow.

> ▸ Approximately 4.5 million Americans have Alzheimer's disease.
> ▸ Twice as many people have Alzheimer's disease today as in 1980.
> ▸ By the year 2050, there may be as many as 16 million people with Alzheimer's disease.

Alzheimer's Disease

1

Anyone can have a lapse in memory. This becomes especially likely as people grow older. It's easy enough for elderly people to forget the names of people they haven't seen in a while or the titles of the books that they read last year. People can expect this as a natural part of aging. But what about someone who no longer recognizes his or her favorite grandchild? Or a person who reaches for a pair of scissors to cut the price tag off a new pair of gloves but can't remember how to hold the scissors in order to use them? For years, people thought that memory loss and confusion were normal phases of old age, but today we know better. Though sometimes it may take an older person longer to recall things, most aging adults remain alert and capable during their senior years.

> Alzheimer's disease is one of the most severe disorders of the brain.

Some individuals, however, are dealing with a brain disorder known as **dementia**. Having dementia seriously interferes with a person's ability to carry out everyday tasks and activities. Alzheimer's disease is the most common cause of dementia.

Labeling objects and rooms in the house can help Alzheimer's patients carry out simple tasks such as hanging up clothes.

Unfortunately, there is no cure for Alzheimer's disease. It's been described as the most severe irreversible memory disorder, and it is the fourth-leading cause of death among older adults. The effects of AD slowly take their toll on an individual, eroding a person's ability to function effectively both mentally and physically. Alzheimer's is most often associated with severe mental impairment, and as it progresses its symptoms go far beyond forgetfulness. The average person with Alzheimer's disease will live for eight to ten years following diagnosis. Some Alzheimer's disease patients have lived for up to twenty years with the disease. The more severe the symptoms at the point of diagnosis, the shorter the patient's survival time is likely to be. Some research also shows that "difficult to manage" patients, especially those who tend to wander or fall, appear to have shorter survival times.

ASK DR. BROWNDYKE

Q: What tests might be ordered to evaluate a patient? How do they help to rule out causes of memory problems other than Alzheimer's disease?

A: *Problems with memory may be caused by many different medical conditions besides Alzheimer's disease. To help determine which type of disorder a person has, the doctor will give the patient a physical and mental examination. The patient and his or her family members will be questioned about the early symptoms and types of problems the patient has had. This history will help the doctor decide which additional tests are needed to make a diagnosis, so that the patient may be prescribed a treatment.*

The doctor may request samples of urine and blood for laboratory tests. These tests will help to rule out physical abnormalities that can cause difficulty with memory, such as liver changes, the presence of high levels of harmful substances (e.g., heavy metals), and some viruses. In addition, the doctor may order a lumbar puncture. A lumbar puncture involves inserting a needle into the patient's back at the base of the spine to remove a small amount of fluid. This fluid, called cerebral spinal fluid, bathes the spine as well as the brain. Some medical conditions may cause too much fluid to be produced, resulting in abnormal pressure on the brain. The fluid will be analyzed to rule out the presence of viruses or infections that directly affect the brain.

Medical conditions affecting memory may cause changes in a person's brain tissue or blood vessels. The structure and blood vessels of the brain may be examined with tests collectively called brain scans. The different types of brain scans are described in more detail on page 26. The results of brain scans aid in determining whether memory loss is related to a stroke, injury, tumor, or changes in the blood vessels. It is very important to exclude causes of memory loss other than Alzheimer's disease, because some disorders have treatments that will restore the patient's memory and other abilities to normal levels.

SYMPTOMS OF ALZHEIMER'S DISEASE

As noted by the National Institute on Aging, Alzheimer's disease symptoms may include:
- ▸ repeatedly asking the same questions;
- ▸ becoming lost in familiar places;
- ▸ being unable to follow directions;
- ▸ getting disoriented regarding time, people, and places;
- ▸ neglecting personal hygiene, safety, and nutrition.

In the end, people with Alzheimer's disease are completely unable to care for themselves.

THE WARNING SIGNS

No two cases of Alzheimer's disease are exactly alike. The illness affects people in different ways and at different rates. Nevertheless, the vast majority of Alzheimer's disease cases share some common identifying characteristics.

Becoming Increasingly Forgetful

People in the early stages of Alzheimer's disease will find themselves becoming increasingly forgetful. At first they may forget appointments or small tasks they meant to do at work. One woman who always remembered the birthdays of all eight of her grandchildren found that it was becoming increasingly hard for her to do this. If she didn't leave notes to herself to remind her to check the calendar, she could no longer guarantee that the presents and cards would go out on time.

In another case, a woman whose father had been a distinguished college professor at a prestigious university first realized that something was terribly wrong when her father began to continually ask her to repeat things. Sometimes she had the feeling that he couldn't remember what was said. That became evident one evening when the woman and her husband invited her father out to dinner. While dining, they spent at least a half hour discussing how much the woman loved the new job she'd just started at an advertising agency. Then later on, as they left the restaurant, her father asked her if she'd found out whether she'd gotten the new ad agency job she'd applied for.

Difficulty with Math and Abstract Thought

People with Alzheimer's disease have difficulty dealing with abstract concepts such as those used in math. This becomes especially obvious when attempting to pay bills or balance a checkbook. Ironically, one woman who'd been a bookkeeper and was in the early stages of Alzheimer's had an especially hard time managing anything to do with money.

Trouble Locating the Word They Want to Use

This is extremely common in people with Alzheimer's disease. Often these individuals have words on the tips of their tongues but just can't remember them. They know what they want to say but are unable to find the right words to express themselves. For example, someone with Alzheimer's may be able to picture a fork in his or her mind and may know that it's an eating utensil with four prongs, but that individual may simply not be able to come up with the word *fork.*

Disorientation Involving Time and Location

People with Alzheimer's disease often become confused about times, dates, or where they are. This tends to worsen as the disease progresses, leaving the affected person frustrated and often extremely upset.

Trouble finding the right words was particularly difficult for the author Jonathan Swift, who wrote the famous *Gulliver's Travels* as well as other books. After developing Alzheimer's disease in his later years, he wrote, "[I can] hardly write ten lines without blunders.... Into the bargain I have not one rag of memory."[1]

WHAT'S IN A NAME?

Dr. Alois Alzheimer, a German physician, identified Alzheimer's disease in 1906. He had noticed specific changes in the brain tissue of a fifty-one-year-old woman who had died of the disorder we know today as Alzheimer's disease. She had experienced severe memory loss and feelings of extreme confusion. She eventually became completely disoriented. While working with the woman when she first came to the hospital, Dr. Alzheimer had asked her to write her name. She tried but failed several times before she looked up at the doctor in frustration and said, "I have lost myself."[2]

In one case a woman who'd been shopping drove her car to her street only to be faced with an unsettling dilemma—she didn't know which house was hers.

Poor Judgment

People who were extremely competent in everything they did prior to the onset of Alzheimer's find that even everyday challenges become difficult for them. One man with Alzheimer's disease, who'd always enjoyed playing card games and checkers with his young grandsons, found that somehow these games had become very complicated. Unable to understand them anymore, he could no longer play the games with the boys. Both he and his two grandsons were robbed of a pleasurable activity that they'd looked forward to on their visits.

Trouble with Routine Chores

Tasks that used to be routine, such as cooking a meal, making a bed, addressing an envelope, or driving a car, become quite challenging for someone with Alzheimer's disease.

DRIVING DANGEROUSLY

Doctors warn that patients with Alzheimer's disease should give up driving cars. This is especially true as the disease progresses and erodes the skill and quick reaction time needed to drive safely. In a study of the effects of Alzheimer's disease on driving, affected individuals often:

▸ missed turns they were instructed to take;

▸ didn't know how to backtrack to reach their destinations;

▸ frequently sped through intersections with their foot on the accelerator.

It isn't safe for those with Alzheimer's disease to drive even short distances in their own neighborhoods. That's because even a familiar environment changes from day to day. It might be a street crew doing road repairs or the way the cars are parked, but there is always something different in our surroundings. A person with AD may not react appropriately to the changes.

Driving is often regarded as an important element of independence, and many individuals with Alzheimer's disease are reluctant to give up their driver's licenses. Some medical professionals believe that frequent mandatory driving tests could prove invaluable in preventing individuals from driving when they are no longer safely able to do so.

Personality and Behavioral Changes

People with Alzheimer's disease usually do not remain even-tempered as the illness progresses. Many experience mood swings and exhibit a broad range of emotions. They may become depressed, anxious, distrustful, frustrated, and restless. In many cases they fear or distrust those around them, even though these people may be trying to help them.

That happened to one woman who went to live with her son and daughter-in-law after being diagnosed with Alzheimer's disease. She believed that everyone in the new household was trying to steal her things. As a result, she would hide her jewelry, money, clothing, and even her false teeth in different places around the house and yard. When she would forget where she put her belongings, she was certain that someone had stolen the items, and this only made tensions in the home worsen.

> **Common Emotions of Alzheimer Patients**
>
> • Depression
> • Anxiety
> • Distrust
> • Frustration
> • Restlessness

WHOM DOES ALZHEIMER'S DISEASE STRIKE?

There are a number of factors known to play a part in determining who develops Alzheimer's.

Age

Age is by far the greatest determining factor in Alzheimer's disease. The older you become, the higher your risk for AD. The Alzheimer's Association states that in people over sixty-five, the number of individuals with Alzheimer's doubles every five years. There are some people between the ages of thirty and sixty who develop what is known as **early-onset Alzheimer's disease**. This is, however, fairly uncommon.

The memory problems caused by Alzheimer's often cause great frustration for those who suffer from the disease.

Family History

There is some data to indicate that people with a family history of the disorder are more likely to develop it themselves. The risk is greater if a close relative such as a parent, brother, or sister has Alzheimer's disease. People who have one close relative with Alzheimer's disease are 3.5 times as likely to develop the disease than those with no such relatives. Their risk for the disease increases with each additional relative who has the illness.

Gender

The available research is not consistent here. There are several studies that indicate women are at a higher risk for Alzheimer's disease than men. There is one large study, however, showing that men are more likely targets for the disorder. It could be that more women than men tend to get Alzheimer's disease because women tend to live longer.

Ethnic and Population Differences

Although far more research is needed in this area, it looks as if African Americans and Latinos are more likely to develop Alzheimer's disease than white Americans. According to the Alzheimer's Association, Alzheimer's is projected to increase six-fold among Latinos in the United States during the first half of the twenty-first century. This increase means that 1.3 million Latinos will have AD by 2050, a huge increase when compared to the 200,000 currently living with the disease. Stephen McConnell, Ph.D., and senior vice president of advocacy and public policy for the Alzheimer's Association, puts it this way, "As the fastest growing population in the country and the group that will have the greatest life expectancy of all ethnic groups, Hispanics will experience a dramatic rise in their risk of Alzheimer's disease."[3] Interestingly, there are lower rates of Alzheimer's disease among Asians as well as among North American Crees and Cherokees than in the overall U.S. population.

> By 2050, 1.3 million Latinos will have Alzheimer's disease.

It's highly likely that environment plays a role in who develops Alzheimer's. One study revealed that the risk of Japanese men developing AD increased significantly after they moved to the United States. This has been shown to be true for other groups as well. Alzheimer's disease is more common among African Americans living in the United States than indigenous people in western Africa.

High Blood Pressure and High Cholesterol

Some research indicates that elderly people with high cholesterol and high blood pressure are at a higher risk for Alzheimer's disease. A portion of this work was done by Dr. Larry Sparks, a forensic pathologist at the University of Kentucky Medical Center, in Lexington, Kentucky. Sparks performed **autopsies** on numerous individuals who'd died unexpectedly. He found that about 70 percent of those who died from heart disease had high cholesterol. After examining their brains, Sparks found that they also had Alzheimer's disease.

Other studies support his findings. Rabbits fed a high cholesterol diet developed the brain changes characteristic of Alzheimer's disease, but reducing cholesterol in their diets lessened this tendency. At this time, however, the connection between high cholesterol and Alzheimer's disease has not been conclusively proven. Nevertheless, when certain cholesterol-reducing drugs were prescribed for elderly patients, these medications appeared to have some protective value against Alzheimer's disease.

Level of Mental Activity

People who remain mentally active are thought to be at lower risk of developing Alzheimer's disease. This is especially true for people who engage in mentally stimulating activities in their later years.

Head Injury

Researchers suspect that there may be a link between serious traumatic head injuries and Alzheimer's disease. This theory grew out of the observation that many boxers develop some form of dementia, but studies on this theory show mixed results so far.

RESEARCH

BOXER'S SYNDROME AND ALZHEIMER'S DISEASE

Research done at the University of Pennsylvania's Center for Neurodegenerative Disease Research showed that the changes that occur in the brains of punch-drunk fighters or those with boxer's syndrome are similar to the changes found in the brains of people with Alzheimer's disease. Such findings suggest that brain injuries may increase the risk of developing Alzheimer's later in life.

Dr. Tracey McIntosh, director of Penn's Head Injury Center, has suggested that even people who seem to fully recover following a head injury might not realize the effects until years later. She noted, "The effects of these self-inflicted brain injuries are not always readily apparent, and we are only beginning to understand the long-term secondary effects of trauma."

ASK DR. BROWNDYKE

Q: What are the general criteria for a diagnosis of probable Alzheimer's disease?

A: *There are many different types of disorders affecting the brain that may cause memory loss. As people age, it is normal to have declines in memory that may become more noticeable in their fifties and their seventies. When the memory loss is much greater than would be expected for an individual's age, then the person may have a type of dementia. Dementia is a general term that means a person has a medical condition resulting in reductions in memory and some other decrease in cognitive (thinking) ability. For instance, he may have reduced ability to speak fluently. The changes must be great enough to affect the person's ability to function at work, home, or in social situations.*

There is no one test that can be given to a patient while he is alive to provide a definite diagnosis of AD. Since many disorders cause memory problems—the primary symptom of AD—other types of conditions are first ruled out. This includes disorders that may worsen over time, such as Parkinson's disease and cerebrovascular disease; medical conditions that may cause dementia, including HIV (human immunodeficiency virus); and substance-induced memory loss (e.g., alcohol). Sometimes a person becomes temporarily confused after taking too much of a medication. For a diagnosis of probable AD, patients must exhibit their problems with memory on a steady basis, rather than during a temporary episode of confusion as might be expected following an overdose of medication.

Patients with probable AD have multiple declines in cognitive functioning, including memory and at least one other type of deficit. For instance, they may have problems identifying familiar objects or persons, speaking, sequencing hand movements to complete daily tasks, and planning or organizing. The combination of these deficits causes significant impairment in the person's ability to function at work, home, or in social situations. The symptoms of AD occur gradually and continue to get worse over time. For a diagnosis of probable AD, memory problems must occur on a regular basis, not only during periods of depression. Sometimes a disturbance of mood or thought is mistaken for a problem with memory. In these cases alleviating the person's depression will also improve his memory. A last diagnostic consideration is when the symptoms of AD occur. If the symptoms occur prior to the age of sixty-five, a diagnosis of early-onset AD is considered.

Hormone Therapy

At one time many American women used hormone replacement therapy to treat the symptoms of menopause. Then, in 2003, it was shown that women who used combination hormone replacement therapy (estrogen plus progesterone) nearly doubled their risk of developing Alzheimer's disease and other dementias.

Down's Syndrome

A large number of individuals with Down's syndrome who reach old age develop changes in their brains that greatly resemble those of Alzheimer's disease.

DIAGNOSIS

There is still no definitive test to detect Alzheimer's disease, although researchers hope that there will be one in the future. Presently, a true diagnosis of Alzheimer's disease can be obtained only through an autopsy in which brain tissue is examined after an individual's death. The National Institute on Aging stresses that physicians are able to make only a "possible" or "probable" diagnosis of Alzheimer's disease while their patient remains alive.[4] Nevertheless, at many specialized medical centers, doctors are correct in their likely diagnoses about 90 percent of the time.

In attempting to diagnose probable Alzheimer's disease, doctors rely on a number of different tools.

A Complete Medical History of the Patient

This gives the doctor overall information on the state of the patient's general health. It covers any past and present medical issues and reveals any difficulties the person is presently experiencing in his or her daily functioning. Sometimes, the patient's caregiver is asked to help provide this information. This becomes especially necessary in cases where the

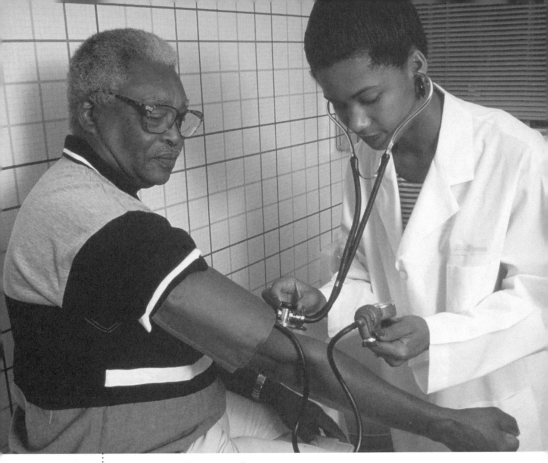

A thorough medical exam should be performed before a diagnosis of Alzheimer's disease is considered.

patient may already be too confused to accurately provide the information the doctor needs.

Medical Tests

The patient is given a broad range of tests in which his or her blood, urine, and spinal fluid are tested and evaluated. The results are often crucial in helping physicians rule out other possible causes for the patient's symptoms.

Brain Scans

Brain scans provide doctors with a close-up view of a patient's brain and, in some cases, allow physicians to tell if something does not look quite right.

Psychological and Neurological Tests

These tests assess the patient's memory, language, attention span, and problem-solving ability. An early diagnosis of probable Alzheimer's disease allows doctors to treat the illness before the symptoms have progressed too far. That diagnosis cannot be arrived at, however, until a thorough evaluation is done to rule out other illnesses with similar symptoms. Conditions frequently mistaken for Alzheimer's disease are:

Conditions Commonly Mistaken for Alzheimer's Disease

- Psychiatric disorders
- Drug reactions
- Poor nutrition
- Aging

Psychiatric and Other Disorders

In some forms of mental illness, patients exhibit intellectual disturbances that may be mistaken for Alzheimer's disease. Individuals suffering from severe depression sometimes resemble AD patients as they increasingly withdraw from social activities. Symptoms mimicking Alzheimer's may also result from a head injury, brain tumor, or stroke.

Drug Reactions

At times, elderly people combine a number of prescription drugs with over-the-counter medications while trying to treat themselves. Unfortunately, the drugs may interact with one another, causing the users to become confused or to experience some memory loss. Older patients in this unsettling mental state have sometimes been thought to suffer from Alzheimer's disease. When taken off the medications by a physician, however, their symptoms disappear.

Alcohol and recreational drugs can yield similar effects to those of medications. Once the substances leave the bloodstream, the individual's memory usually returns to normal. Prolonged alcohol and drug

ASK DR. BROWNDYKE

Q: What are the different types of brain scans that may be done?

A: *There are several types of tests that may be used to better understand what is going on inside the brain. Some medical conditions affect the structure of the brain, while others may lead to changes in blood vessels or functioning. Each type of brain scan provides different information. The patient's physical and cognitive (thinking) symptoms will determine which type of brain scan will be done.*

Computerized tomography (CT) provides X-ray pictures that show the structure of the brain. A CT scan may reveal changes such as tumors or an abnormal buildup of blood. CT scans tend to cost less and to be collected faster than other types of brain scans such as magnetic resonance imaging (MRI). MRI is similar to CT in that it also shows pictures of the structure of the brain. The benefit of MRI is that the pictures are clearer than the fuzzier-looking CT scans. MRI can also expose smaller changes that may not be apparent with a CT scan, such as a small stroke or changes in the structure of the blood vessels.

Magnetic resonance angiography (MRA) gives a picture of the blood vessels in the brain. There are both large and small blood vessels located throughout the brain. Though blood vessels may look normal, a medical condition sometimes causes a change in the amount of blood flow in certain areas of the brain. This may be detected with single photon emission computed tomography (SPECT). The location of the reduced blood flow may suggest a particular condition. Positron emission tomography (PET) is similar to SPECT in that it can measure blood flow. In addition, PET may also be used to show whether certain nutrients and natural brain chemicals are being used normally. It can also help doctors determine if some areas of the brain are not getting enough of these substances. The image on the next page compares the PET image of a patient with Alzheimer's disease with that of a healthy person of similar age.

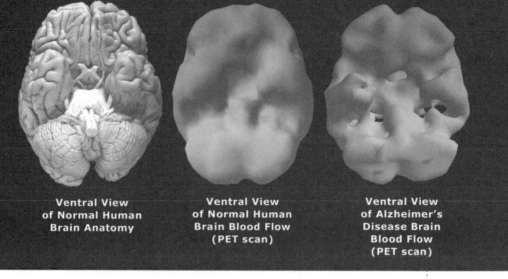

The restricted blood flow in the brain of an Alzheimer's patient is apparent when the patient's PET scan is compared to the scan of a brain with normal blood flow.

abuse, however, can permanently affect a person's thinking and memory.

Poor Nutrition and Metabolic Changes

Poor eating habits and changes in the way the body functions can cause an individual to experience symptoms common to Alzheimer's disease. Unlike those with Alzheimer's, however, individuals in these situations readily improve with appropriate treatment.

Aging

In some cases, the physiological changes and memory loss associated with aging are mistaken for the onset of Alzheimer's disease. Yet there are distinct differences between the two conditions. In Alzheimer's, major changes in memory interfere with everyday life and the person's ability to function.

Researchers are working on a number of indicators to allow them to distinguish between patients with Alzheimer's disease and those with other conditions. A recent conference funded by the National Cancer Institute underscored the evidence that shows that chemotherapy treatments for some forms of cancer can produce long-term cognitive changes. The number of cancer survivors is increasing, so it is important to be able to differentiate between chemotherapy-related changes in the brain and those produced by Alzheimer's.

Other studies point to intriguing new clues that may one day prove to be important indicators of Alzheimer's disease. Some work has revealed that changes in a person's sense of smell may actually be an early sign of Alzheimer's. In one such study, a large number of older Americans were asked to smell various items as part of an odor identification test. Two groups of people took part in the study—one group consisted of healthy older Americans, while the other was made up of older people believed to have Alzheimer's disease. During the testing, investigators measured activity levels in the regions of the brain that control the sense of smell. They found that those suspected of having Alzheimer's disease showed a decreased level of brain activity in these areas.

The 2003 Progress Report published by the National Institute on Aging noted the following:

Insights from these and many other studies will help scientists understand the natural history of Alzheimer's disease and the ways in which changes in memory and other cognitive functions differ in normal aging, AD, and other dementias. This knowledge will help clinicians diagnose AD earlier and more accurately and will also help researchers pinpoint early changes that could be targets for drug therapy.[5]

THE IMPORTANCE OF AN ACCURATE DIAGNOSIS

Securing an accurate diagnosis and getting medical help is crucial for those with Alzheimer's disease. When that doesn't occur, the consequences can be tragic, as they were in the case of the Canadian filmmaker Claude Jutra, who had enjoyed success both in his native country and abroad.

Because of his reputation as a man of expansive vision and keen analytical ability, coworkers and film critics were perplexed when Jutra started to become exceedingly absent-minded and disorganized. Claude Jutra developed his own ways of coping. He tape-recorded important conversations and ideas and kept a list of what needed to be done each day. He also posted additional reminders to himself throughout his home and office.

As time passed, Claude Jutra drifted into a somewhat solitary existence. Because he had trouble remembering people's names as well as expressing himself, social interactions frustrated him. Seeing him increasingly cut off and isolated, friends were relieved when Jutra's younger sister moved in to care for him. Jutra had sought medical assistance for the problem, but it was 1986 and diagnostic techniques were not as sophisticated as they are today. Unfortunately, the physicians he saw weren't very helpful. At the urging of some friends and former colleagues, Jutra and his sister sought out new specialists.

Eventually Jutra's sister found a respected psychiatrist who agreed to see her brother. After a three-hour examination and thorough assessment of his medical history, the physician arrived at a diagnosis of probable Alzheimer's disease. As the illness is incurable, Jutra's sister was given a bleak prognosis: following a slow mental and physical deterioration, Claude would contract an infection or illness that would result in death.

Jutra's regression was difficult for those close to him to watch. He suffered from insomnia and frequently paced through his house at night. With the passing months, Claude Jutra grew even more tortured by his surroundings. Unfortunately, he was still lucid enough to realize that things would worsen for him. One day in November 1986, Jutra told his sister that he was going out for a walk. She thought nothing of it since he often went out alone, but it turned out to be the last time she saw him alive. Despite a lifelong fear of heights, Claude Jutra jumped from the railing of the Jacques Cartier Bridge into the St. Lawrence River. Determined not to accept an end imposed on him by Alzheimer's disease, he chose his own.

After his drowning, a small notebook containing messages Jutra had left for his family and friends was recovered. Considering his condition, it contained a remarkably clear account of his illness's progression and the feelings that led to his suicide. The following excerpts reveal some of what he experienced:

August 1981 — I'm losing my memory. At work, I'm constantly repeating myself. I have to transcribe everything that's said; otherwise it's as if I never heard it.

October 26, 1986 — I'm certain now that I suffer from Alzheimer's disease. There's nothing I can do. It's set in motion and there is no stopping. Some of those who are close to me know the truth. But I don't know if they suspect that I know.

October 29, 1986 — For a long time now I suffer horribly from anxiety. Waves of panic engulf me without reason. Those attacks last several minutes and leave me.

October 30, 1986 — I read things that I have written at different moments of my life, and I realize the difference in quality, in vitality. I amaze myself that I can even understand what I'm writing now. If I'm not careful, I will fall into a horrible trap. I must act before it is too late. . . . Perhaps darkness is another kind of light. I hope so.[6]

All About Alzheimer's Disease

Martin and Anna were high school teachers who'd been married for more than forty-five years. Before they retired two years ago, they'd made lots of plans. Anna wanted to write children's books, while Martin was going to spend his time woodworking and reading. The couple thought that their golden years would be the best years of their lives. Unfortunately, they were mistaken. That's because, following their retirement, Anna was diagnosed with probable Alzheimer's disease.

Anna never got to enjoy the retirement she had dreamed of. She never wrote children's books as she had planned. Once, while she was still lucid enough to realize what was happening, she told Martin that she felt as if she were being robbed. Anna realized that Alzheimer's disease was stealing her mind.

THE AGING BRAIN VERSUS THE BRAIN AFFECTED BY ALZHEIMER'S DISEASE

At times, some of the physiological changes and memory loss associated with the onset of Alzheimer's disease have

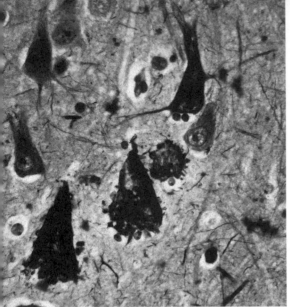

Alzheimer's disease damages cells in the area of the brain known as the cerebral cortex.

been mistaken for aging. This was the case with Anna and Martin in the early stages of Anna's illness. Yet there are distinct differences between the two conditions.

In Alzheimer's disease memory problems quickly worsen and are sometimes compounded by other symptoms. While the memory loss associated with normal aging largely tends to be moderate and gradual, Alzheimer's disease results in a complete erosion of the individual's mental faculties. In Alzheimer's disease, major memory changes get in the way of ordinary living and the ability to function.

There are also distinct differences between the brain of an aging person and the brain of someone with Alzheimer's disease. An autopsy performed on a person who suffered from Alzheimer's disease reveals specific changes in the brain resulting from the illness. It usually shows that the brain has shrunk somewhat and that there has been a loss of **neurons,** or nerve cells, from an area considered essential to processing thought. Scientists have also found extensive clusters of damaged nerve endings known as **beta-amyloid plaques** in the brains of people who had the disease. These dense plaques are largely made up of deposits of protein and cellular material. Another hallmark of Alzheimer's disease is nerve cells containing twisted fibers called **neurofibrillary tangles.** While elderly people may develop some plaques and tangles, those with Alzheimer's disease develop significantly more of them.

ASK DR. BROWNDYKE

Q: What is cerebral atrophy?

A: *The human brain may shrink slightly as we age. When the amount of shrinkage is more than would be expected based on the person's age, it may be a signal that there is something wrong. Medical conditions, such as Alzheimer's disease, may result in loss of brain tissue. This loss of brain tissue is called cerebral atrophy. There may be general atrophy seen throughout the brain or atrophy only in specific areas of the brain. The tissue loss is actually a reduction in the number of cells. Brain tissue is made up of neurons, and other cells that support the structure of the brain. When the atrophy becomes fairly extensive, there is a decline in cognitive abilities. The exact symptoms will vary depending on the location of the atrophy. The reduction in cognitive abilities may be caused by the loss of brain tissue or the disruption of connections between areas of the brain.*

In AD, cerebral atrophy may first become apparent in certain regions of the brain, including some that are very important when trying to learn new information. As the disease advances, the amount of atrophy apparent in a CT scan or MRI is greater and may be visible over large areas of the brain. The image below compares the brain of a healthy person to the brain of a patient with the cerebral atrophy that is typical of Alzheimer's disease.

Brain Atrophy Characteristic of Alzheimer's Disease on a Magnetic Resonance Imaging (MRI) Scan

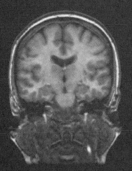
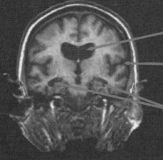

enlarged ventricles

wider gaps between folds in the cortex

prominent atrophy in the hippocampus

Unaffected 70-year-old

Affected 72-year-old

In addition, Alzheimer's disease alters some brain **neurotransmitters,** the chemical messengers through which nerve cells communicate. Among these is **acetylcholine,** a neurotransmitter crucial to memory. In short, Alzheimer's disease interferes with normal cell action. As nerve cells in the brain stop functioning properly, they lose connections with other nerve cells and eventually die. The result is the memory loss and other problems associated with Alzheimer's disease.

NOT A NEW PROBLEM

It is highly likely that Alzheimer's disease had affected older individuals for many years before it was first identified by Dr. Alois Alzheimer in 1906. Scholars have pointed out that Shakespeare was probably describing the ravages of Alzheimer's disease in his play *King Lear*. In this production, an aging king feels abandoned by his daughters as his faculties diminish. In the following passage from the play, the king describes what he believes is happening to his mind:

{ Alzheimer's disease is the result of a series of events, occurring over a period of time, within the brain.

I fear I am not in my perfect mind.
Methinks I should know you, and know this man;
Yet I am doubtful; for I am mainly ignorant
What place this is; and all the skill I have
Remembers not these garments; nor I know not
Where I did lodge last night. Do not laugh at me.
—King Lear, *Act IV, Scene 7*

CAUSES OF ALZHEIMER'S DISEASE

What causes Alzheimer's disease? This is one of the most pressing questions asked of doctors who treat patients with the disease. It's often the first thing anyone affected by the illness wants to know. Unfortunately, at this time, there are no clear-cut answers. Some diseases, like chicken pox or pneumonia, have readily definable causes and can be prevented or cured with vaccines or antibiotics. But this is not the case with Alzheimer's.

Alzheimer's disease is thought to be the result of several factors that interact and cause the disease process to start. There is no set formula. The importance of each factor may vary among individuals. While scientists still don't fully understand the reasons involved in the development of Alzheimer's disease, they know that the disorder results from a complex series of events occurring in the brain over a long period of time. Some of the factors suspected of being involved in this process are discussed below.

The Gene Factor

It's been noticed that Alzheimer's disease seems to run in some families, and in recent years scientists have done a great deal of detective work to learn the possible role **genes** or heredity play in this disorder. Did people from families in which Alzheimer's disease was common share some genetic trait? The gene factor seemed particularly relevant in early-onset Alzheimer's, and after some investigation the researchers' work centered on **chromosomes** 1, 14, and 21.

Scientists learned that some families have a mutation in some of the genes on these chromosomes. These abnormalities are an important factor in the development of the disease. A person is highly likely to develop early-onset Alzheimer's even if just one of these genes inherited from a parent has a mutation. Therefore, the child of a couple in which one parent has the gene mutation has a 50 percent chance of developing early-onset Alzheimer's disease.

It is important to remember that early-onset Alzheimer's disease is relatively rare and mutations in these three genes have nothing to do with late-onset Alzheimer's disease. Through research, however, scientists have isolated another gene whose presence does indicate an increased risk for **late-onset Alzheimer's.** The molecular version of the gene is a common protein known as **apolipoprotein E,** or APOE. This

EARLY-ONSET ALZHEIMER'S DISEASE—SPECIAL PROBLEMS

Though the symptoms of early-onset Alzheimer's disease are quite similar to those of late-onset Alzheimer's, people who develop this disorder before they are sixty-five are often faced with some unique problems. This is largely because of the way the disease impacts a middle-aged person as opposed to someone who's well advanced in years.

Individuals with early-onset Alzheimer's are far more likely than older people to be employed at the time their symptoms surface, and many will be parents of teenage, or even younger, children. Since any dementia is not expected in younger people, their symptoms are often mistaken for psychiatric problems or a lack of motivation. Rather than be given help for a medical problem, they are more likely to be fired from their jobs for poor performance. Sometimes these individuals find that they have to leave their jobs because they are no longer able to function effectively in them.

The subsequent loss of income can lead to serious financial problems for their families. Unfortunately, individuals under sixty-five are often ineligible for some medical benefits and social-support programs. They must frequently obtain special waivers to receive these benefits and services.

Having dependent children at home when this type of the disease strikes can create quite a few problems. Children who once depended on the parent for homework help, financial support, and guidance will no longer be able to do so. They'll need help in understanding what's happening to their father or mother. They'll also need to learn to cope with the everyday changes that will dramatically affect their lives. The situation often becomes especially difficult for the spouse of someone with early-onset Alzheimer's. These spouses are usually younger and still in the workforce. At a time when money is badly needed to keep the family going, they may not be in a position to leave work to care for their spouses and children full time. Families affected by early-onset Alzheimer's often find that they require a lot of support from outside sources.

protein, which normally assists in transporting cholesterol in the blood, has three forms. One of these, known as **APOE-4,** was found in significant amounts in the brains of many deceased late-onset Alzheimer's disease patients.

Researchers are still unsure of APOE-4's precise role in Alzheimer's, but it is present in about 40 percent of patients who develop the disease. A study revealed that the protein appears to bond tightly to a substance within the plaques found in the brains of Alzheimer's patients. Dr. Blas Frangione, a molecular biologist at New York Uni-

Alzheimer's patients must often rely on family members to help them remember things and complete daily tasks.

versity Medical Center, found that the protein hastens the development of similar plaques in laboratory cell cultures. Additional research is needed to learn more. In commenting on the complexity of the disease and its possible origins, Frangione noted that while APOE-4 is a factor in late-onset Alzheimer's disease, not everyone with APOE-4 will develop the disorder.

Additional research indicates that other genetic factors may be involved in late-onset Alzheimer's disease. In 2002, the National Institutes of Health published *Alzheimer's Disease: Unraveling the Mystery*. In this publication, three teams of scientists using three different strategies reported that chromosome 10 has a region that may contain several genes that could increase a person's risk of AD. Identifying these genes is one important step in the research process that will lead to a new understanding about the ways in which changes in protein structures cause the disease process to begin and about the sequence of events that occurs as the disease progresses. Once they understand these processes, scientists can search for new ways to diagnose, treat, or even prevent AD.[1]

Beta-Amyloid

Much recent Alzheimer's disease research has centered on **beta-amyloid,** an abnormal protein found in the brains of Alzheimer's disease patients. Beta-amyloid is a fragment of a normal protein, APP, that occurs in soluble form in various parts of the body. Unfortunately, in Alzheimer's a still unexplained malfunction causes APP to split in an unusual way, triggering the release of beta-amyloid.

Scientists initially thought that beta-amyloid was a product of the disease, but now they feel it may play a role in how the illness ravages the brain. In one animal study, beta-amyloid was injected into the brains of rats. Although the injections did not precisely duplicate Alzheimer's disease in rodents, the animals experienced a type of brain cell death similar to that of patients with AD. The work was significant because it established a direct connection between beta-amyloid and neuron destruction in living animals.

The researchers came up with other exciting results as well. They found that another brain protein, known as substance P, acted to prevent the induced brain damage in rats. Substance P is a neurotransmitter present in the normal brain, but it is typically deficient in the brains of those with Alzheimer's disease. When injected directly into the rats' brains, either with the beta-amyloid or alone, it reduced toxicity and prevented cell death and the appearance of antibodies similar to those found in people with AD. The scientists also noted that the positive results were directly related to the amount of substance P used—the higher the dosage, the better the outcome.

Although these findings are promising, more work needs to be done. Scientists hope to learn precisely how beta-amyloid affects the nerve cells of people with Alzheimer's disease.

Tau

In recent years, scientists have been looking at **tau** as a possible factor in Alzheimer's disease. Tau is a protein found in the nerve cells of the brain. In people with Alzheimer's disease, however, this protein behaves differently—it gathers in tangled filaments in the neurons. Researchers have found that these tau abnormalities are present in other degenerative brain disorders as well.

Cardiovascular Risk Factors

Some studies point to a possible link between risk factors for heart disease and those for Alzheimer's disease. Studies on mice at the University of Washington in Seattle showed a direct connection between

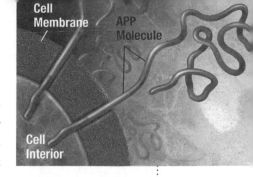

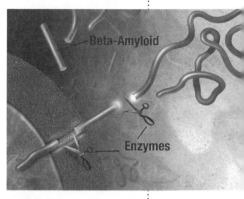

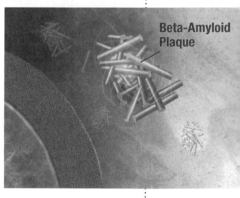

When molecules of the protein known as APP break down, beta amyloid is formed. The beta amyloid creates the plaques that are characteristic of Alzheimer's disease.

> **The Healthy Adult Brain**
>
> **Size:** A normal adult brain is about the size of a medium cauliflower.
>
> **Weight:** The brain weighs about three pounds (1.4 kilograms).
>
> **Number of nerve cells (neurons):** 100 billion

high cholesterol levels and the risk for Alzheimer's disease. Animals in the study that were fed a high cholesterol diet developed high levels of cholesterol in the blood and brain and increased beta-amyloid deposits. A number of researchers have also found that statins, the drugs used to lower cholesterol and reduce the risk of a heart attack, may also lower the risk of developing AD. The same appears to be true for high blood pressure (hypertension). Even in relatively healthy older adults, having high blood pressure increases the risk for stroke, heart disease, and Alzheimer's disease.

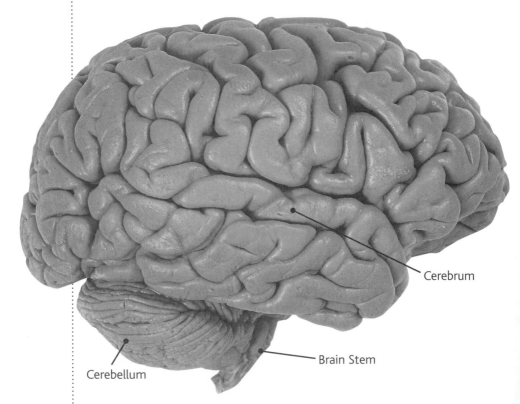

Cerebrum

Brain Stem

Cerebellum

The human brain is composed of three main parts: the cerebrum, the brain stem, and the cerebellum.

Oxidative Damage from Free Radicals

This is a fairly new and promising area of investigation. As noted by the National Institute of Aging:

This theory suggests that, over time, damage from a kind of molecule called a free radical can build up in neurons, causing a loss in function. Free radicals can help cells in certain ways, such as fighting infection. However, too many can injure cells because they are very active and can readily change other nearby molecules, such as those in the neuron's cell membrane or in DNA. The resulting molecules can set off a chain reaction, releasing even more free radicals that can further damage neurons. This kind of damage is called **oxidative damage.** *It may contribute to AD by upsetting the delicate machinery that controls the flow of substances in and out of the cell.*[2]

Inflammation

Inflammation is another possible factor in Alzheimer's disease. Inflammation is a function of the immune system that affects tissues and cells in all parts of the body. Inflammation can occur in response to a tiny cut as well as with a disease like rheumatoid arthritis that can affect a person's entire body. Signs of inflammation in the body include redness and swelling, among others.

In examining the plaques found in the brains of deceased patients with Alzheimer's disease, scientists have come across various cells and compounds associated with inflammation. As a result, they believe that inflammation may play a role in AD, though at this time they aren't sure just what that role is.

It's interesting to note that scientists don't agree on whether the inflammatory process may be helpful or harmful when it comes to Alzheimer's disease. Some scientists think that it may be of value in assisting the brain in clearing away beta-amyloid deposits. Others believe that it may trigger a vicious cycle that could possibly damage neurons in the brain. These scientists are basing their assumptions on research like the Honolulu-Asia Aging Study. In this study, aging in Japanese American men was tracked over a number of years. It was found that those who had higher levels of C-reactive protein (an indicator of inflammation) in their blood at midlife had an increased risk of developing Alzheimer's disease twenty-five years later. At this time, though, more research is needed in this area.

Aluminum Accumulations
In the 1960s, scientists learned that aluminum could be detrimental to the brains of rabbits. It was later found that the brain cells of some people with Alzheimer's disease contained unusually high levels of aluminum. Yet, at this time, it is not known how these accumulations relate to the disease. Does the aluminum cause or contribute to the illness in some way? Or is it an end result of Alzheimer's?

There are also other factors involved. Scientists have sometimes found high aluminum levels in the brains of healthy older individuals as well as those with AD. In addition, an individual's environment can influence the amount of aluminum in his or her body. In certain areas of the country where the aluminum soil content is denser than average, all the residents tend to exhibit higher aluminum levels. Though a number of studies have been done through the years to investigate this connection, there have been contradictory findings. At this point, most scientists feel that if aluminum is a factor in Alzheimer's disease, it's not a highly significant one.

THE STAGES OF ALZHEIMER'S DISEASE
The deterioration characteristic of Alzheimer's disease doesn't happen all at once. Instead, it's a slow process that begins with changes occurring in the affected person's

The first stage of Alzheimer's is often mistaken for the forgetfulness that is often considered a normal part of the aging process.

brain long before there are noticeable changes in thinking and behavior. Alzheimer's disease is a progressive illness, which means that the person's condition worsens with time. The following is a brief description of the three presently recognized stages of the illness.

Stage 1

The first stage of Alzheimer's disease is largely characterized by memory loss concerning recent circumstances or events. For example, people in the early stages of the disease might repeatedly forget the names of friends or colleagues,

- Stage 1 lasts two to four years.
- Stage 2 lasts two to ten years after diagnosis.
- Stage 3 lasts one to three years.

where they put the car keys, or the zip code of their hometowns. Times, dates, and appointments sometimes become scrambled in the person's mind.

At first these memory lapses may be of little concern, because at times everyone forgets things. In an Alzheimer's disease patient, however, memory loss increases and usually extends to numerous areas of the person's life. As the problem intensifies, it becomes difficult for the individual to deny that something is seriously wrong.

ASK DR. BROWNDYKE

Q: How are the cognitive symptoms of Alzheimer's disease tested?

A: *When a doctor sees a patient suspected of having AD, he or she will give a brief test of mental abilities, such as the Mini-Mental State Exam. If the patient has severe deficits, the changes in memory and other abilities can be easily determined. But if the declines are relatively mild, it may not be clear whether the changes in cognitive abilities are normal for a person's age or more extensive and a possible harbinger of more severe declines. In these cases, the doctor may refer a patient for a neuropsychological evaluation.*

Neuropsychologists are psychologists who specialize in studying brain behavior relationships. They assess patients with standardized measures—tests that are based on normative data, which means that many healthy normal controls of different ages and educational levels have been given these tests before. Their scores are used to determine what normal and abnormal performances are. For example, their scores may be used to determine whether a certain score is within the impaired, low average, average, high average, or superior range.

When a patient is referred for suspected dementia, the neuropsychologist administers a battery of tests designed to assess functions such as memory, abstract thinking, executive functioning (e.g., ability to alternate between different types of responses), speech, attention, intellectual abilities, spatial skills, and motor speed. The pattern of strengths and weaknesses across the test profile is examined for consistency with a specific type of dementia or normal aging. If Alzheimer's disease is probable, the neuropsychological evaluation also helps to determine the stage of the disease, that is, early, middle, or late AD.

The first neuropsychological evaluation may be used to establish a baseline for the future. If further cognitive decline is suspected, the patient can be tested again and the results can be compared to the first evaluation. In this way, the physician can document the progression of the disease. The neuropsychological evaluation also includes evaluation of symptoms of depression, which may make an individual appear as though he has significant problems with memory when he really does not.

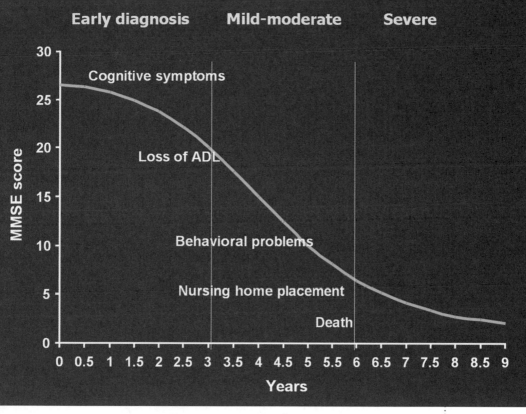

This graph shows the relationship between Mini Mental Status Exam (MMSE) scores and the progression of Alzheimer's disease.

In addition to memory lapses, Alzheimer's disease patients experience language problems. Even those who in the past were fluent conversationalists often find that they can't think of the word or phrase they wish to use. People in the beginning stage of Alzheimer's disease also frequently undergo dramatic mood swings. They may feel frustrated or depressed a good deal of the time and may suffer from insomnia. As the stricken individuals become increasingly embarrassed at their slipping intellectual and interpersonal skills, they may become increasingly withdrawn and avoid social contact whenever possible. Because physical abilities do not begin to decline until later in the disease, patients in the first stage of AD may appear to be healthy. As the months pass, however, they find it increasingly hard to make sense of the world around them.

Other common changes that occur during the early stage of Alzheimer's disease include:

- repeatedly asking the same question;
- becoming confused about direction and having difficulty getting to even familiar places;
- forgetting to pay or overpaying at stores and restaurants;
- misplacing things after putting them away in strange places for safekeeping;
- experiencing personality changes, such as becoming frustrated, suspicious, or more easily upset;
- being less sensitive to the feelings and needs of others than in the past;
- hesitating to try new things;
- making poor decisions with regard to money;
- exhibiting a shortened attention span and experiencing difficulty completing tasks or listening to others;
- becoming easily upset if rushed or if something unanticipated occurs.

During the first phase of Alzheimer's disease, affected individuals often realize that they are losing much of who they once were. The poignant quote at left is from a man named James Thomas who died at age seventy after struggling with AD for eight years. He wrote these words in his daily journal soon after being diagnosed with the illness he referred to as "God's cruel joke."

> I am hungry for the life that is being taken away from me. I am a human being. I still exist. I have a family. I hunger for friendship, happiness, and the touch of a loved hand. What I ask is that what is left of my life shall have some meaning. Give me something to die for! Help me to be strong and free until my self no longer exists.
>
> J.T.[3]

Stage 2

The middle stage of Alzheimer's disease tends to be the longest. In

Alzheimer's patients in the middle stage of the disease need assistance with everyday tasks and cannot live alone.

some cases it lasts for a number of years. The initial symptoms of the disease become decidedly more pronounced. At this point, the stricken patient may vividly recall something that occurred twenty years ago, yet not remember what he or she did the day before.

During this period, the patient may display unusual eating habits and experience restlessness, hyperactivity, and general feelings of frustration. At times, these Alzheimer's disease patients appear panicky for no apparent reason and experience hallucinations and paranoia. There is frequently a sharp decline in personal hygiene, and the individual may need help with such everyday activities as dressing, eating, and using the toilet. At this stage, few Alzheimer's patients are able to live alone and, in the majority of cases, they need full-time supervision.

Other characteristics typical of this period in the Alzheimer's disease patient's life include:

- having difficulty recognizing familiar people and items, for example sees his own car and thinks it belongs to someone else;
- having a shortened attention span;
- becoming very sloppy or disorganized;
- experiencing difficulty bathing or showering alone;
- dressing inappropriately, such as insisting on wearing shorts to a wedding;
- being unable to think through problems or complete tasks effectively;
- wandering outside and being unable to find his or her way back home;
- becoming easily angered and may accuse or threaten;
- being unable to cope with new or unexplained situations;
- experiencing increased restlessness, especially in the late afternoon or at night;
- exhibiting loss of impulse control—person may increasingly use vulgar language or become nasty or menacing to others.

Stage 3

In the final stage of Alzheimer's disease, the patient's learned abilities and memory skills have completely eroded. He or she may find it exceedingly difficult to articulate even the simplest need or desire. During this stage of AD most individuals are no longer able to control bodily functions and many experience seizures.

The ill person continues to decline mentally and physically until his or her body becomes susceptible to an infection or disorder that results in death. In the end,

Alzheimer's disease seems to create a general collapse of a person's bodily systems, making the individual vulnerable to illnesses such as pneumonia or decreased motor skills that can result in problems such as choking on food.

LEONARD'S STORY

Leonard and his wife, Jane, owned a home in Sun City Center, a retirement community on Florida's west coast. Leonard had been diagnosed with Alzheimer's disease about five years before and Jane had done her best to take care of him despite having a heart condition along with some other serious health problems. Jane tried never to leave Leonard alone, but one morning she had to go to the hospital for some tests and the woman she'd hired to watch Leonard had to leave before Jane could get back. Thinking it was all right to leave Leonard alone for an hour or two, the caregiver Jane had hired went on to her next job. It was a terrible mistake. When Jane returned home later that day, the house was empty. Having no idea where Leonard was or if he was all right, Jane phoned the police. They told her to stay where she was in case Leonard came back and said that they'd send a car out to look for him.

Meanwhile, Leonard had been wandering around the mazelike streets of Sun City Center for the past hour. Though he had originally set out to find Jane, he had become confused as to where Sun City Center's hospital was. Now Leonard wanted to go home but couldn't return because he'd forgotten where he lived as well.

After another hour of walking the streets in the hot sun, he wandered onto the back porch of a home and sat down and cried. The owners of the house heard him, and when they saw how confused he was, they called the local police for help. The police car that had been out looking for Leonard arrived, and the officers took him home. Jane was grateful that her husband wasn't hurt, but it was a frightening day for everyone concerned. Unfortunately, as time passed there were many more like it.

Other characteristics that frequently occur during the last phase of Alzheimer's disease include:
- being unable to recognize family members and close friends;
- speaking nonsense or stops speaking altogether;
- experiencing difficulty walking or even standing alone;
- experiencing weight loss;
- sleeping much of the day;
- developing frequent infections.

ASK DR. BROWNDYKE

Q: How does the loss of cognitive functions relate to changes in the brain?

A: *The changes in cognitive abilities associated with AD occur gradually over time. This often makes it difficult for the patient or family members to pinpoint when the first symptoms began. This pattern of gradual change is different from that found in other types of dementia that have a sudden onset of symptoms. For example, patients with vascular dementia, or decline in memory associated with disruption of blood flow, may report having sudden symptoms that may or may not get better with time. The steady, more gradual decline noted in AD is associated with changes in certain areas of brain tissue.*

Initially, there may be a decline in memory that is not substantial enough to be considered diagnostic of Alzheimer's. This stage may be called mild cognitive impairment. If a person continues to decline, he or she may be considered to be in to the early stages of Alzheimer's. The changes are most likely the result of a reduction in size of areas of the brain that are very important in memory—the hippocampus and a nearby region called the entorhinal cortex. The loss of tissue in these regions is associated with an increase in the senile plaques and neurofibrillary tangles that are the hallmark of the disease.

As the disease advances to the middle and later stages of AD, repeated brain scans typically show a noticeable reduction in brain tissue over larger areas of the brain. The ventricles (spaces containing fluid inside the brain) usually become enlarged, and there is a corresponding loss of tissue in the temporal and parietal lobes of the brain. These regions are important to memory, to some aspects of language such as naming objects, and to spatial abilities. At this point, patients may demonstrate difficulty copying simple geometric designs. Even prior to reductions in the structure of temporal and parietal areas, there are changes in the amount of blood flow and uptake of nutrients with positron emission tomography (PET).

PERSONALITY, MOOD, AND BEHAVIORAL CHANGES

The personality and behavioral changes that accompany Alzheimer's disease can be extremely distressing to the family and friends of those affected by the illness. As the disease advances, these individuals often become demanding, behave childishly, make insulting remarks, become inappropriately sexual, and even become violent. People who were once tactful, pleasant, and easy to get along with may now seem combative, stubborn, and agitated a good deal of the time. The problem can become even more extreme if the person with AD experiences delusions and hallucinations (seeing and hearing things that are not there).

It's important to remember that people with Alzheimer's disease don't want to be this way—their behavior is a direct result of their illness. The complex processes that take place in a healthy person's brain are seriously disrupted in someone with the disorder. Besides wiping out memory, Alzheimer's also erodes prior learned behaviors regarding good manners and getting along with others. Some of the anger and agitation often exhibited by people with AD also comes from the frustration of not being able to express themselves or do things they once accomplished with ease.

The same is true for the clinging or shadowing behavior frequently displayed by people with Alzheimer's disease. Here, formerly independent individuals may not want to let their caregivers out of their sight for a moment. This is because the world has become a strange and frightening place in which they can't remember the past and have no idea of what to expect in the future. Remaining constantly close to a trusted caregiver may provide their only sense of security in an increasingly confusing world.

The same disruption in thinking accounts for much of the other socially unacceptable behavior frequently seen in people with advancing Alzheimer's. On a very hot day, a

A trusted caregiver often provides a sense of security to an Alzheimer's patient whose world has become increasingly confusing and frightening.

person with AD might begin to take off all his or her clothes, just as someone else might remove a sweater. Both people feel warm, but the person with Alzheimer's disease doesn't remember that it's unacceptable to publicly disrobe.

Nevertheless, coping with these behaviors can prove challenging for the person's loved ones. One woman took her father, who had Alzheimer's disease, to live at her home when she felt that he was no longer capable of caring for himself. She did everything she could to make his life with them as comfortable as possible. This included filling his room with sports memorabilia, which she hoped would bring him pleasure.

Though her father had been a talented salesman before he'd retired and knew how to get along with all kinds of people, Alzheimer's disease had robbed him of these skills. Now his temper often flared when he couldn't find something he wanted or if someone in the family insisted that he do something he didn't want to do—such as taking a bath. He'd also loudly curse, and even though his daughter had asked him to try not to do this in front of her children, he seemed unable to stop himself.

It was his loud cursing that once sent his daughter and her husband rushing up to his room in the middle of the night. Apparently he had become delusional. They found him yelling all sorts of things while urinating on the night-light plugged into the wall near him. He thought it was a fire and he was trying to put it out.

Though caregivers may understand that the irrational and bizarre behavior exhibited by their loved ones is a result of the disease, it can still be unnerving. Some families even feel that the behavioral problems exhibited by people with Alzheimer's are harder to deal with than the memory loss most often associated with the disease. As one woman whose "kind and gentle" husband became "cunning" and "aggressive" after his disease had progressed stated, "The behavioral changes I've seen are absolutely frightening. . . I was afraid of him." She went on to describe the overall effect of these personality changes on loved ones as follows: "Most families won't talk about it. I equate this disease to how leprosy used to be. We've lost good friends and we have family members who won't have anything to do with us. I think they're afraid of it, and there's a real stigma that the person is crazy. I think it's why a lot of families hide people away who have it."[4]

Alzheimer's Disease: A Forgotten Life

Treatment

At four o'clock in the afternoon she [his wife, Stella] looked into my workroom and said dinner was ready. Dinner at four o'clock in the afternoon? Maybe for farmers? Maybe for people in Iowa? I was still working. Maybe she had misread the time. She was standing beside me. I looked at her wristwatch. Four. I showed her my desk clock. Four. She was unimpressed. Dinner was ready. I pointed out the window to the light that hung on in the January afternoon. The sky was white; the colors of roofs and fields could be made out. At our usual dinner hour, neighborly window lights would break the darkness. This was not very interesting to her. Dinner was ready. . . . Stella saw nothing irregular about dinner at four and was irritated when I asked her to cover my plate, I would microwave it later. I was working.[1]

The story above reflects a spouse's growing realization that something is terribly wrong with his wife. Soon enough he'd learn that he was probably losing his wife to Alzheimer's disease. As people and their spouses receive that dreaded diagnosis, they are always anxious to know what can be done to help their loved ones.

MEDICATIONS

Unfortunately, Alzheimer's disease is incurable. There is
no way to completely stop it or reverse the damage that it
does. In recent years, however, a number of new medications have been developed for people in the early to middle
stages of AD. Though these drugs may stop some symptoms from worsening, they work only for a limited period
of time. Yet to people with Alzheimer's and their families,
even a short respite on the path to total incapacitation is
treasured. The drugs currently being used for this purpose
are Aricept (donepezil), Exelon (rivastigmine), and Remenyl (galantamine). Cognex (tacrine) is another drug in this
family used by people with Alzheimer's disease, but it is no
longer actively marketed by its manufacturer.

These medications are known as cholinesterase inhibitors. At this time scientists still aren't sure precisely why
these drugs are effective, but recent research may have
provided some important clues. It's suspected that these
medications prevent the breakdown of a brain chemical called acetylcholine. Acetylcholine is vital to memory,
thinking, and reasoning. As the years pass and Alzheimer's
disease advances, however, the brain manufactures reduced
amounts of acetycholine. That may be why cholinesterase
inhibitors stop working after a while.

There are no available studies that compare the various cholinesterase inhibitors' effectiveness, so it's impossible to say which drug has been most successful in helping Alzheimer's disease patients. Since all these drugs
work similarly, it's unlikely that changing from one drug
to another would produce a dramatic improvement in any
patient. Because of his or her individual body chemistry,
however, a patient may sometimes respond better to one
drug than another.

There's only one medication that is usually prescribed

*Some medications can help slow the progress of Alzheimer's, but there is
no drug that can cure the disease.*

to help patients with moderate to severe Alzheimer's disease. This drug is known as Namenda (memantine) and is used to delay further deterioration in people with AD. Patients taking the medication sometimes retain the ability to control their bodily functions for a few months longer, and that can be quite helpful to the individuals and their families.

Namenda works differently from the cholinesterase inhibitors. It controls another important brain chemical called glutamate. Excessive amounts of glutamate produced by the brain can lead to brain cell death. Since Namenda's

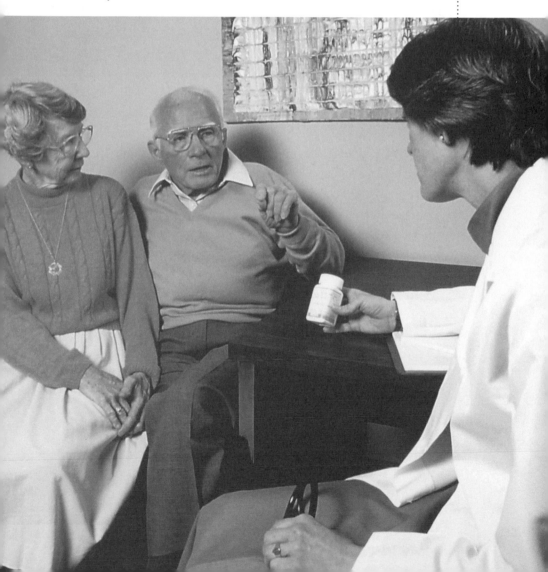

STRUGGLING TO SURVIVE

The new cholinesterase inhibitors sometimes allow people in the early stages of Alzheimer's to stay on the job longer. These medications, however, are not miracle drugs, and the people taking them often find they have to devise additional coping techniques to help them survive in the work world. That was the case with one high-energy New York City advertising executive who had recently been diagnosed with AD. This executive had been known for his especially creative ad campaigns, and for years he'd always had brainstorming sessions with his staff in which everyone threw out their ideas for the campaign under discussion. Because of the disease, that casual and creative approach no longer worked for him. The ad executive found that he couldn't remember the ideas put forth and integrate them into a winning strategy. He still held brainstorming sessions with his staff, but now any idea given serious consideration in the session had to be submitted to him in writing the next day. He told his staff that this was necessary, because the firm was growing larger and they needed to be more organized. They didn't know that the real reason was that this was the only way their boss could continue to function on the job.

action differs from that of the cholinesterase inhibitors, in some cases doctors prescribe both types of drugs in combination for patients who might benefit from taking them.

Patients taking any of the drugs for Alzheimer's disease must be monitored by a physician. Often the doctor starts the patient out on a low dosage to see how well that person tolerates the medication. If all goes well, the dosage can be increased. All these drugs have some side effects. Common side effects of cholinesterase inhibitors include nausea, vomiting, diarrhea, and weight loss. Namenda may cause dizziness, headaches, and constipation.

In addition to the drugs, which have been specifically formulated for Alzheimer's disease, doctors sometimes prescribe different medications to help with other symptoms of the illness. These are usually **psychotropic medications** or "mind affecting" drugs used to alter emotions and problem behavior. Among these are **antipsychotic medications**, which help prevent violent reactions, restlessness, and hallucinations. Antidepressants have also been frequently

ASK DR. BROWNDYKE

Q: How does excessive glutamate lead to cell death in the brain?

A: *Glutamate is an amino acid that acts as a neurotransmitter in the brain. Neurotransmitters allow the brain to send a message from one cell to another. Glutamate is among the most common brain neurotransmitters, particularly in regions that are vitally important to learning and memory, including the hippocampus located in the middle of the brain. Too little or too much glutamate in this region may result in reduced ability to learn new information.*

Several different medical conditions can cause excessive levels of glutamate, including seizures, strokes, and AD. Too much glutamate in certain areas of the brain leads to what is known as programmed cell death, or apoptosis. There are a number of theories that attempt to explain why this occurs more frequently in AD. One of the most likely theories is that the neurofibrillary tangles that are found in AD trigger the production of excessive amounts of glutamate, leading to cell death. Another theory is that there is a failure of the normal mechanisms that act to remove glutamate, leading to an excess that causes cell death. One drug used to treat AD, called memantine, reduces the excessive levels of glutamate found in the brain in the middle and later stages of AD.

prescribed to help patients who experience mood swings and a tendency toward withdrawal and isolation. Some psychotropic drugs calm overly anxious patients, while other drugs are given for limited periods of time to assist patients with sleep disturbances. Without medication, these patients often experience difficulty sleeping through the night, and in the early hours of the morning they may wander aimlessly through their homes or even out into the street.

ASK DR. BROWNDYKE

Q: What are hallucinations and delusions?

A: *Hallucinations are sensations that seem very real to the person having them, but do not actually occur. Hallucinations may be perceived in any of our senses—hearing, taste, sight, touch, and/or smell. Several different types of mental disorders and neurological conditions may cause hallucinations. Auditory hallucinations often involve hearing voices, when these voices do not exist. People who hear voices may imagine that the voices are telling them to do things that are distressing. Antipsychotic medications are often prescribed to control these hallucinations. Auditory hallucinations occur in some types of dementia but are more common in thought disorders that begin in younger individuals.*

Hallucinations involving olfaction, or sense of smell, may accompany a certain kind of seizure disorder. These patients may smell burning rubber, when it is not present, immediately before an episode of convulsions, or shaking. Tactile hallucinations involve the sensation of being touched in some way that is not happening. For example, drug abuse may cause the sensation of something crawling on the skin. Visual hallucinations are more likely to accompany AD than other types of hallucinations. A patient may believe that he or she sees small people, when there are no people there. This is more likely to occur in situations where there are shadows in the evening.

Patients with AD may have delusions as well. Delusions are similar to hallucinations in that they are not real, but delusions are false beliefs rather than sensations. Patients with AD may be prone to delusions, particularly in the middle stages of the disease. For example, a patient may misplace a possession, and instead of realizing he has lost the object, he may believe that someone entered his home and stole it. Or a patient with dementia may become jealous and have the false belief that her spouse is being unfaithful.

Although psychotropic drugs can be used to normalize a person's behavior, they have drawbacks. Medicating older patients with these drugs requires meticulous physician supervision. An elderly person's body generally consists of more fat and less protein than a younger individual's, and some psychotropic drugs are readily drawn into the body's fatty tissues. As a result, less medication reaches the brain. Drugs stored in the patient's body fat also take longer to exit the body when medication is discontinued.

In addition, the body's sensitivity to medications increases with age, and the brains of AD patients are frequently especially sensitive to drugs. In many instances, even small amounts of psychotropic drugs have significant effects.

Not all doctors automatically prescribe psychotropic drugs for their Alzheimer's disease patients. Some find that changing a patient's daily routine, providing new forms of stimulation, and eliminating daytime naps are more beneficial to the restless patient than medication. In the early stages of the disease, counseling can be useful. Even as the disease progresses, patients may benefit from recreational time spent with supportive friends and relatives. As new and improved medications specifically formulated to treat Alzheimer's disease are developed, there may be less call for psychotropic drugs.

AN ACTIVE AREA OF RESEARCH

Researchers are actively involved in developing new drugs that might prevent Alzheimer's disease, slow its advance, and reduce the severity of its symptoms. One exciting discovery in this area was announced by the National Institutes of Health in the fall of 2004. Researchers had identified a protein named **transthyretin** that may prove useful in halting the progression of AD. It seems that transthyretin protects brain cells from the deterioration caused by Alzheimer's by blocking the toxic protein beta-amyloid. Transthyretin may preserve brain cells by intercepting the beta-amyloid and preventing it from disabling nerve cells and producing memory loss.

"Based on the results of the animal studies, we know that the disease process depends in large part on the delicate balance between the 'good' transthyretin protein and the 'bad' beta-amyloid," noted Dr. Jeff Johnson, associate professor at the University of Wisconsin's School of Pharmacy and the lead author in that study. "In Alzheimer's patients, the 'bad' protein significantly outnumbers the 'good' proteins."[2]

Johnson's transthyretin work grew out of a study involving mice that had received defective genes responsible for early-onset Alzheimer's disease from human patients. The defective genes produced mice with higher-than-normal levels of the toxic beta-amyloid protein—just as the researchers had thought it would. Yet they were amazed to find that the mice did not exhibit Alzheimer's symptoms. As Johnson put it: "We have a mouse whose brain is bathing in toxic beta-amyloid without exhibiting disease symptoms. We were all asking the same question—Why aren't these cells dying?"[3]

After analyzing the brains of the mice, they found dramatically increased levels of transthyretin. "We concluded that the transthyretin must have protected the brain cells from the toxic effects of the beta-amyloid," Johnson explained.[4] The next step was to see if the same would hold true for humans. So the researchers conducted test-tube studies with brain cells cultured from a human cortex. The brain cells were treated with transthyretin protein, then exposed to beta-amyloid. The brain-cell death was minimal. "Now that we have demonstrated that this protective mechanism is relevant to humans, we can start to identify strategies to stall nerve degeneration in Alzheimer's patients," Johnson concluded.[5]

In Their Own Words: A Person with Alzheimer's Disease

A sense of utter helplessness swept over me when the doctor said that I probably had Alzheimer's disease. The very words Alzheimer's disease sounded harsh and unreal. I wanted to believe that he was talking about someone else—not me.

I remember asking a few questions. Was he sure? Could it be something else? What could he do for me? I remembered how he leaned forward and stayed close to me when he answered, but I don't remember what he said. I did not want to listen.

I wanted to talk; but I didn't want anyone to know how scared I was. I had always imagined myself to be a strong person who could face anything. But now I was afraid of a disease I did not understand. How was I going to live the rest of my life and take care of my family? All I could see was darkness.[6]

DIET AND NUTRITION

According to researchers at Yale–New Haven Hospital, a healthy diet is not only important for people with Alzheimer's disease, but it may also prove to be a vital factor in preventing the disorder. Research has shown that a diet that includes vitamins known as **antioxidants** may help to lower a person's risk for developing disease. Vitamins E and C are believed to be especially important. Vitamin E is found in both vegetable and nut oils, in addition to whole grain products and spinach. Vitamin C is found in citrus fruits such as oranges, grapefruits, lemons, and pineapples. Vitamin C is also present in spinach, tomatoes, and peppers.

FRUITS AND VEGETABLES RICH IN ANTIOXIDANTS INCLUDE:

avocados	lemons	strawberries
blueberries	mangos	sunflower seeds
broccoli	oranges	wheat germ
cantaloupe	peppers	whole grains
collards	pineapples	
kale	spinach	

Another valuable measure in warding off Alzheimer's disease is having a low cholesterol diet. Animal products such as meat, eggs, poultry, and dairy all contain cholesterol. Very high levels of cholesterol in the blood are thought to nearly triple a person's risk of developing Alzheimer's disease.

ASK DR. BROWNDYKE

Q: What is atherosclerosis, and how is it related to Alzheimer's disease?

A: *Atherosclerosis refers to a buildup of plaque, or fatty deposits, inside the walls of the large blood vessels called arteries. When 20 percent or less of the diameter of the artery is reduced by atherosclerosis, the atherosclerosis is classified as mild. In some cases, however, atherosclerosis is more severe, causing a reduction of 50 percent or more of the diameter of the artery. Significant buildup such as this causes the blood flow in the artery to be reduced. Pieces of plaque may break off and travel to other areas of the body. If the plaque blocks an artery that feeds the heart, it can cause a heart attack. If the plaque blocks an artery leading to the brain, it may induce a stroke. A stroke is a sudden severe disruption of blood flow, resulting in symptoms such as sudden difficulty with speaking or being unable to move one side of the body. Sometimes an operation can be performed to reduce plaque in the two large blood vessels running up the sides of a patient's neck to prevent a stroke from occurring.*

Atherosclerosis is associated with Alzheimer's disease. The buildup of fatty deposits in atherosclerosis is related to the development of abnormalities in the brain such as neuritic plaques and neurofibrillary tangles. Thus, the presence of significant atherosclerosis suggests that an individual may have plaques and tangles in the brain as well. This is an important marker for these brain abnormalities, since we cannot tell from an MRI or a CT scan whether plaques or tangles exist.

There are several risk factors for the development of atherosclerosis, including smoking cigarettes, high cholesterol, high blood pressure, obesity, and diabetes. Atherosclerosis tends to become significant as we age, but it may begin in childhood and worsen over the course of a patient's lifetime. These findings emphasize the importance of eating healthy foods, getting regular exercise, and avoiding cigarette smoking.

FISH RICH IN OMEGA-3 FATTY ACIDS INCLUDE:

halibut	sardines
herring	trout
mackerel	tuna
salmon	

Eating fish, which has sometimes been referred to as a "brain food," has also been shown to be highly beneficial. This is because omega-3 fatty acids, which are found in fish, have been shown to reduce the risk for Alzheimer's disease. This finding was confirmed in three separate scientific studies at Tufts University in Boston, Rush University in Chicago, and the University of California at Los Angeles.

Shannon Adkins, whose mother was diagnosed with Alzheimer's disease at just fifty-two years old, is eating more fish these days. Shannon first realized that there was a problem when she happened to be in the car while her mother was driving on a multilane highway. All of a sudden, her mother simply took both her hands off the wheel. Luckily Shannon, who was in the passenger seat, managed to grab hold of the wheel and steer the car to safety.

Shortly after that incident, her mother was diagnosed with Alzheimer's disease. Five years later, Shannon's mother was no longer able to eat or dress on her own. Shannon described how her mother's life had dramatically changed. "It's a very different life now," Adkins noted. "She [her mother] spends a lot of time confused. She doesn't know where she is or who she's with."[7]

Although Shannon Adkins can never mend her mother's mind, she's now including more fish as well as fruits and vegetables rich in antioxidants in her own diet. It's a small measure to take that might help prevent Shannon from developing Alzheimer's when she grows older. As

Engaging in physical activity, such as gardening, can be very helpful for Alzheimer's patients.

Ernst Schaefer, a researcher at Tufts University, put it, "I listen to people talk about Alzheimer's and they say, 'Nothing works,' but the data suggest that Alzheimer's might be a disease that one can prevent."[8]

EXERCISE: PHYSICAL AND MENTAL

Some degree of physical activity may be extremely beneficial while a person with Alzheimer's disease is still mobile. Walking, jogging, gardening, or playing Ping-Pong may be good choices, depending on the person's physical con-

MAINTAIN YOUR BRAIN

The Alzheimer's Association is actively encouraging everyone to be more aware of the risk factors involved in Alzheimer's disease. Their "2004 Maintain Your Brain Campaign" is part of this effort.[9] The campaign urges everyone to adopt a "brain-healthy lifestyle" by following the suggestions below:

1. Head First: Good health starts with your brain. It's one of the most vital bodily organs and needs care and maintenance.

2. Take Brain Health to Heart: What's good for the heart is good for the brain.

3. Your Numbers Count: Keep your body weight, blood pressure, cholesterol, and blood sugar levels within recommended ranges.

4. Feed Your Brain: Eat less fat and more antioxidant-rich food.

5. Work Your body: Physical exercise keeps the blood flowing and may encourage the growth of new brain cells. Do what you can, such as walking thirty minutes a day to keep both body and mind active.

6. Jog Your Mind: Keeping your brain active and engaged increases its vitality and builds reserves of brain cells and connections. Read, write, play games, learn new things, do crossword puzzles.

7. Connect with Others: Leisure activities that combine physical, mental, and social elements may be most likely to prevent dementia. Be social, converse, volunteer, join a club, or take a class.

8. Heads Up! Protect Your Brain: Take precautions against head injuries. Use your car seat belts, unclutter your house to avoid falls, and wear a helmet when cycling or Rollerblading.

9. Use Your Head: Avoid unhealthy habits. Don't smoke, drink excessive amounts of alcohol, or use street drugs.

10. Think Ahead—Start Today! You can do something today to protect your tomorrow.

dition and personal interests. Exercise can improve the individual's attitude and feelings of well-being. Sometimes physicians recommend exercise regimens for patients with Alzheimer's disease who have difficulty sleeping through the night.

When devising an exercise program for someone with Alzheimer's disease, it's important to have realistic expectations. If, after the disease progresses, a walk around the block is too much for the person to handle, try a walk around the yard instead. It's important to be aware of any signs of overexertion and encourage the patient not to do more than he or she is capable of.

Regularly scheduled exercise has also been shown to lower a person's risk of developing Alzheimer's disease. Staying active mentally can reduce the risk as well. This can be done by doing mental tasks that require memory and reasoning skills. Doing crossword puzzles, playing Scrabble, and reading books are all good choices.

> **BE AWARE!**
>
> In 1983, President Ronald Reagan designated November as Alzheimer's disease month. This was before he developed the disorder. By declaring November to be Alzheimer's month, he hoped to raise public awareness about this devastating illness.

OTHER PREVENTION METHODS

There are other measures that can be taken to reduce the risk of Alzheimer's disease. Not smoking is high on the list. The harmful substances in cigarette smoke can damage blood vessels and possibly brain cells. It's thought that this may lead to various forms of dementia, including Alzheimer's disease. Drinking small amounts of red wine (no more than two small glasses a day) can be helpful, but the key here is moderation. Too much alcohol increases a person's risk for AD.

Alzheimer's Disease: A Forgotten Life

Caring for Someone with Alzheimer's Disease

4

There have been many stories about how difficult it can be to care for someone with Alzheimer's disease. One of the most highly publicized cases was that of Roswell "Ross" Gilbert, who on March 5,1985, shot his wife of fifty-one years, claiming he could no longer tolerate what Alzheimer's had done to her.

Throughout the Gilberts' long marriage, friends and neighbors had thought of Ross as a loving, doting husband who enjoyed pampering his wife and indulging her whims. While Ross owned only a single suit, he made certain that his wife was always well dressed and never felt deprived. As a neighbor described the situation, "Emily was a pampered woman. She had an off-white fur coat, a leopard coat, and a fur stole. She liked to shop and play bridge, but she never made a meal in her life. Ross made his own coffee in the morning and then they ate out."[1]

When Emily Gilbert was stricken with Alzheimer's disease, her husband took care of her by

> People caring for someone with Alzheimer's disease need to know as much as they possibly can about the illness.

himself, choosing not to worry other family members with their problem. He also wanted as few people as possible to know about his wife's condition, to spare Emily any embarrassment.

That meant that as the disease advanced, he had to bathe and dress his wife and apply her makeup every day. He even brushed her teeth and gave her an enema most mornings since she was often constipated. When Emily became completely incontinent, Ross Gilbert changed her diapers.

Ross tried to keep his wife calm because she frequently became agitated or enraged without provocation. It was not unusual for Emily to ask Ross the same question twenty or thirty times a day. Each time he would try to respond lovingly and patiently. "Ross never raised his voice to Emily," a close family friend observed. "But, oh, he must have been embarrassed. It was an impossible situation."[2]

At times, Emily's condition became especially trying. Once she broke several ribs in a bad fall. Although Emily hated hospitals, Ross had to take her to one because she needed immediate medical attention. After arriving, Emily became disoriented and began running up and down the halls, disturbing the other patients. When the hospital staff finally subdued her, gave her a sedative, and put her to bed, Ross refused to leave his wife. He spent the night sleeping fully clothed on the floor alongside her bed.

But Emily awoke the next morning even more upset than she had been the previous day. She began running through the hospital corridors again, claiming that she needed to locate the elevator buttons before she could sit down. Although she was wearing a dress, she didn't seem to notice that her stockings were falling down around her ankles. Because she had already been treated for her broken ribs, there was little else the hospital could do for her. Exhausted by the events of the past two days, Ross took his wife home.

In the days ahead Emily was inconsolable. She was distraught and in pain because of her broken ribs and told a neighbor that on numerous occasions she had contemplated suicide. She added that she and Ross had made a pact long ago not to let each other suffer. Shortly after that conversation, she arrived at Ross's office looking upset and claiming she didn't want to go on living. Ross calmly ushered her out of the building and took her home. She sobbed all the way back and was still crying as she rested on the living room sofa.

At that point Ross, apparently feeling that it was unfair to let his wife go on this way, loaded his shotgun and fired two bullets into Emily's brain while she was on the couch. Moments later he stepped into the hall of his condo and told a neighbor, "I just shot Emily. . . . Somebody had to do it."[3]

Roswell Gilbert was arrested and tried for the murder of his wife. Friends and neighbors of the Gilberts were shocked when the seventy-five-year-old man was found guilty of murder in the first degree and sentenced to twenty-five years in prison. His supporters claimed that he had merely rescued his wife from what Ross had referred to as her torturous "descent into a living hell."

Obviously the jury viewed the circumstances differently. It apparently decided that Roswell Gilbert had killed his wife to free himself from the ongoing burden of Alzheimer's disease. Although Emily Gilbert's illness had measurably hampered her level of functioning, there were still many things she was capable of enjoying. The jurors wondered whether Emily was genuinely aware of the trying nature of her often-erratic behavior. The defense argued that Emily had been in great emotional pain, but the jury ultimately saw Ross as not only unbearably tormented by his wife's illness but willing to go to extremes to solve the problem. Ross Gilbert remained in prison for five years. Then he was granted clemency and released due to his failing health.

Another reaction to the advanced stages of Alzheimer's disease became evident on a Saturday evening in Post Falls, Idaho, when a custodian at Coeur d'Alene Greyhound Park, a dog racetrack, came across an abandoned elderly man in a wheelchair in the grandstand after closing. The man wore a baseball cap, sweat suit, and blue bedroom slippers. A note taped to the side of his wheelchair identified him as John King, a retired farmer suffering from Alzheimer's who was in need of round-the-clock nursing care. The labels had been cut out of his clothing and all identifying marks removed from the wheelchair. It was obvious that the man had been abandoned there and that his family did not want him traced to them.

Abandonment is not unusual among families emotionally and financially drained from caring for relatives with Alzheimer's and related illnesses. "It's shocking and terrible," noted former University of Chicago geriatrician Dr. Christine Cassel, "but it doesn't surprise me at all. The families of Alzheimer's disease patients sometimes just give up in despair."[4]

Dr. Cassel's assessment was echoed by Chicago emergency room physician Dr. Cai Glushak, who has seen desperate relatives leave people with Alzheimer's disease in emergency room corridors and not come back for them. "It happens here probably once a month," she said. "Before you can turn around, the person who registered the patient is gone. They've left no phone number, no address."[5] And sometimes the people who abandon the ill are not always relatives. At times the elderly sick person has no relatives or they live far away, and he or she is left to the mercy of strangers by landlords or even household employees. While it's difficult to secure reliable statistics on this distressing phenomenon, some have estimated that between one hundred thousand and two hundred thousand patients are deserted annually at hospital emergency rooms.

ASK DR. BROWNDYKE

Q: What is apraxia, and how does it affect activities of daily living (ADL)?

A: *Apraxia refers to the inability to complete voluntary movements in a functional manner. This is an acquired condition that is not due to problems with muscles or sensation. It may become especially apparent when the patient needs to use or manipulate an object with the hands. For example, a person may be unable to tie shoelaces or button clothing. Sometimes a patient is able to complete such tasks, but it requires much more effort and time than usual. In this case it would be considered dyspraxia, because there is reduced ability, rather than complete loss of ability to perform a function. To test whether a patient has this difficulty, a doctor may ask a patient to imitate the hand movements necessary to use a key to open a door or to cut something with scissors.*

Apraxia or dyspraxia may accompany a number of neurological conditions, including head trauma, strokes, and brain tumors. Though apraxia commonly occurs with AD, it typically does not become evident until the later stages of the disease. It may make coordinating and sequencing the movements needed to complete such basic activities as dressing and bathing exceedingly difficult. Some patients may be unaware that they have this difficulty, but their family members notice that it takes more time for them to get dressed. Once they are dressed, patients may be unaware that a shirt is on backward or is buttoned incorrectly. These types of difficulties may be compensated for by choosing shirts without buttons and shoes without laces.

As it turned out, the man left at Coeur d'Alene Greyhound Park was actually John Kingery, an eighty-two-year-old former autoworker who lived more than three hundred miles from the Idaho dog track. Because there is no Idaho law against abandoning the elderly, authorities faced a unique dilemma. "To me it's a sin and crime," said Post Falls detective Harlan Fritzsche, "but I'm left in a quandary [as to what to do about it]."[6] So are a growing number

It is difficult for an elderly person to care for a spouse with Alzheimer's disease, especially if the caregiver has health problems of his own.

of people who must come to terms with the physical, emotional, and financial needs of a loved one with AD.

Despite the media attention focused on cases of abandonment, murder, and suicide, the families of Alzheimer's disease patients and the patients themselves seldom resort to such extreme measures. While Alzheimer's is undeniably trying for everyone involved, most individuals find constructive ways to cope with this irreversible, incurable illness. Some families have found it helpful to identify existing positives within their dilemma and to build on these.

Identifying positives and building on them can be extremely important for caregivers helping a person with AD. Being responsible for someone with this illness can take a tremendous physical and emotional toll on anyone in this role.

WHO ARE THE CAREGIVERS?

According to the National Institute of Aging, most of the people who care for individuals with Alzheimer's disease are family members.

Spouses make up the largest group of caregivers. Unfortunately, this is sometimes a problem in itself. That's because many of these people are also elderly, and trying to handle their own health problems while caring for a husband or wife is difficult.

Daughters make up the second largest group of caregivers for people with AD in the United States. These women are often married and raising families of their own. Many have jobs outside the home as well. At times, these women are referred to as being in the "sandwich generation." That's because they are frequently pulled between the responsibilities of caring for their children and those of caring for their parents.

Daughters-in-law make up the third largest group of family caregivers for people with Alzheimer's. They find themselves in the role of helping to care for their husbands' parents.

Sons tend to be more involved with the financial, legal, and business aspects of caregiving. Though some may help with the day-to-day dressing, bathing, and meal planning and preparation for an older family member with AD, sons are more likely to take over banking and bill paying for the individual. They are often the ones who ensure that the person's will and funeral plans are in order.

At times, brothers and sisters have become involved in caring for a sibling with Alzheimer's disease. This is especially true if they live nearby and have enjoyed a close relationship with their sibling. Often siblings are in the same age range, however, and at times these caregivers have their own health problems to contend with. Many siblings become too frail to accomplish all that's needed in these situations.

Depending on their age at the time they are needed, grandchildren can sometimes help with the care of a grandmother or grandfather with Alzheimer's. In cases where the grandchildren still actively need the care of their own parents, however, they may need help in accepting that much of their parent's attention has become focused on the grandparent. Depending on the situation, friends, relatives, and mem-

ASK DR. BROWNDYKE

Q:
How does Alzheimer's disease affect a person's ability to drive?

A:
Driving a car is a very complex activity when it is broken down into all its component parts. It requires adequate vision, hearing, and the ability to respond rapidly to situations that arise. In addition to sensation, perception, and motor skills, driving requires using these abilities to perform higher cognitive functions such as visual memory, visual attention, and knowledge of how far to turn the steering wheel to stay on the road. A driver must be able to sequence hand and foot movements.

Reaction time is the length of time required to respond to a stimulus. As we age, reaction time slows, even in completely normal individuals. This can be tested in a laboratory by having someone press a button on a computer keyboard when he see a specific object on the monitor. In everyday life, reaction time may translate to responding quickly by stepping on the brake when an animal or child darts out in front of the car. In patients with AD, reaction time is slower than in other adults of the same age.

People with normal mental abilities learn, with practice, to coordinate all the usual activities involved in driving. In individuals with AD, however, these activities become dangerous for many reasons. They may lack visual attention, memory, or both, and become lost in previously familiar surroundings. Every once in a while there is a story in the news about an elderly driver who accidentally hit a person who was walking near his car. This is sometimes blamed on accidentally stepping on the accelerator rather than the brakes, but the incident may be related to the symptoms of AD. No one wants to give up the privilege of driving. If there is concern about whether or not a person should be driving, a doctor can refer the patient for a driving evaluation. The evaluator will specifically test the person's driving ability and identify related safety issues.

As Alzheimer's disease progresses, patients often become unable to feed themselves and must rely on caregivers to feed them.

bers of a person's church, synagogue, or mosque may become involved in the care of someone with Alzheimer's disease.

CAREGIVER RESPONSIBILITIES

At first a caregiver may just be involved in cooking meals for the person with Alzheimer's disease, paying his or her bills, and taking that individual to doctor and dentist appointments. As the illness progresses, however, affected individuals usually require significantly more help. Many become easily agitated or upset and need someone to calm them. At this point such individuals often have to be bathed, dressed, and fed as well. With advanced Alzheimer's, people frequently become too ill to be left alone for even short periods, and continuous nursing care becomes necessary.

Coping with the personality changes and decreased mental abilities of a loved one requires a lot of patience. Tasks that a person could handle a few months ago may become too complex and challenging. Caregivers have been known to get upset over what they see as the inherent unfairness of a disease that robs a loved one of being who he or she once was. As one woman whose husband had AD described it:

> *I cannot believe that God let my husband survive Hitler to get this disease. He was the only one in his family not to be killed by Hitler's army. My Joe was a good man who lived for me, his children, and his congregation.*
>
> *Now, even with Alzheimer's disease, he still goes to worship each day. I do not know how many of the prayers he still understands, but of one thing I am sure. Joe finds inner peace and comfort there. One Saturday he came home and sat down with me for dinner. I prepared to say the blessing when he reached for my hand and kissed it: "My lips cannot say the words," he said, "but you know my spirit fights to speak. I must fight to worship in a silence that goes beyond words."* [7]

Some caregivers find the role changes that occur in Alzheimer's particularly difficult to deal with. It's hard to watch a parent who was once knowledgeable and a dependable source of sound advice reach a point at which he or she no longer recognizes family members. In addition, such tasks as dressing, bathing, and preparing meals for someone with Alzheimer's disease can be physically exhausting.

At times, caregivers become overwhelmed by what they are facing and can be at risk for depression and various illnesses themselves if they don't receive adequate help from family, friends, and the community. Many caregivers find that the key to coping with these circumstances lies in developing flexible strategies to handle the situation. Learning these strategies involves some of the following elements.

Learn All You Can about Alzheimer's Disease

People caring for Alzheimer's patients need to know as much as they possibly can about the illness. This is crucial so that they know what to expect and how to handle hard-to-manage situations. Today, there is quite a bit of good information available on the illness, and much of it is free. Caregivers can contact groups such as the Alzheimer's Association for this data. In many parts of the country, community groups offer classes on working with elderly sick people. These can be extremely beneficial.

Establish a Routine

Working out a day-to-day routine when caring for someone with Alzheimer's disease can benefit both the caregiver and the patient. Caregivers often find that there are particular times of the day when the person seems less confused and more cooperative, and the daily routine can be geared to make the most of these times.

It is also important to learn how to help the Alzheimer's patient while allowing him as much independence for as long as possible. This can be achieved by observing what the person is still able to do and providing opportunities for the person to do it. For instance, if someone with AD finds it hard to use eating utensils, prepare finger foods whenever possible. Using straws or cups with lids can help reduce spills. If a person has trouble choosing what to wear, lay clothes out in advance. Sometimes it's helpful to arrange the clothes in the order that they are to be put on. When purchasing clothes for someone with Alzheimer's disease, it's important to pick comfortable items that are easy to get on and off. Elastic waists and Velcro closures can eliminate struggles with buttons and zippers.

Laying out clothing in advance can help Alzheimer's patients dress themselves. This allows them to have some measure of independence and dignity.

ASK DR. BROWNDYKE

Q: What is sundowning?

A: *Sundowning refers to the tendency of patients with some types of dementia, such as Alzheimer's disease, to be brighter and more capable of tasks at the beginning of the day. These patients become increasingly disoriented and less functional as it becomes dark at nightfall. They may be more likely to become lost and to have problems recognizing people, places, or things. Patients with sundowning become confused, more irritable, and less able to cope. This agitation is thought to be related to not recognizing their surroundings and a subsequent feeling of anxiousness.*

Tiredness and the inability to see well because of darkness and shadows seem to make sundowning worse. It may help to keep a night-light or low-level light on in their rooms at night. If they are in a place that is not their home, it sometimes helps to bring pictures or other familiar objects along.

Wandering is a common behavior that may stem from disorientation. Individuals with AD and other forms of dementia may wander when they are unable to communicate their needs. Wandering can be very dangerous because patients may leave their home, hospital, or other protected environment without any knowledge of where they are going and without adequate or appropriate clothing. They may believe they are following a pattern of behavior that they had for many years, such as going home from work at the end of the day. Another reason patients wander is to try to reorient themselves. The facility where a patient is staying may place a monitoring device on the patient in order to protect him. The device will sound an alarm if he tries to leave. When a patient lives at home, bells can be placed on doors to warn family members that the person is leaving.

Find a Support Group

Caregivers almost always benefit from being in a support group with other people in similar situations. In these groups, people get together to share experiences and to offer advice and support. Support groups can assist in easing the feelings of being overwhelmed or isolated that caregivers frequently develop. They offer encouragement and realistic solutions to get caregivers through especially hard times or difficult decisions. Support groups help caregivers feel they are not alone—others share their concerns.

One man whose wife had Alzheimer's disease described a particularly trying situation that he'd been through to his support group. His story was important to the others there. It let them know that everyone who loves someone with this disorder faces similarly difficult predicaments. He said:

I would like to tell the story of the day Stella and I were driving through Pennsylvania on the way to visit her sister. It was soon after her Alzheimer's had been diagnosed. Stella had stopped driving and I had turned in her license. I pulled off four-lane Interstate 80 to call ahead to the motel to let them know our arrival time.

"I'm only going to make a phone call to the motel [he told his wife]. I'll be back in a couple of minutes. Stay in the car. I'll be right back."

I was beginning to give such instructions firmly and repetitively. When I completed the brief call to the motel and returned to the street, she was gone. The car was gone. She wouldn't know where she was. She would have no idea where she was going. She wouldn't be able to explain driving without a license.[8]

The police were called, and luckily the man's wife and car were safely found less than a mile away. Hearing about experiences like that in a support group setting helps others realize that they are not the only ones forced to cope with these things.

Online support groups are available for caregivers who don't live near a traditional support group or who have trouble finding someone to watch their loved ones while they are gone. These groups have the added advantage of being available around the clock and, as seen in the case cited below by the National Institute on Aging, this can be extremely beneficial:

It was midnight, the end of a long day of taking care of her husband. She was exhausted but she couldn't sleep. A year ago she would have felt totally alone, unable to share the hardships of caregiving, and desperate for ideas for how to cope better with his changeable moods and withdrawal from the world. Tonight was different. She went to the living room, switched on her computer, and plugged into a computer-based support group for family caregivers. She sent out a message and soon received replies from several fellow caregivers. They knew just what she was feeling. Their words of understanding and support eased her mind and helped give her the strength she needed for the days ahead.[9]

Find Help with the Workload

No one individual should be expected to care for a loved one with Alzheimer's disease without help. It's important to involve other family members in sharing this task. Sometimes different family members are responsible for the ill individual on different days of the week. In other situations, family members who do not have the time to physically care for a sick loved one or who live far away may be able to assist financially. The money they contribute can make it possible to hire outside help for a number of hours weekly and provide some time off for the primary caregiver. It's also important to investigate adult day care services that may be available in the area.

Think Ahead and Plan for the Future

Unfortunately, people with Alzheimer's disease do not get better. As the disease advances, their condition worsens. It is important to investigate long-term care options such as nursing homes and to know what expenses may or may not be covered by various health plans and Medicare.

THE POSITIVES AND NEGATIVES OF CAREGIVING

There are both positive and negative aspects of caring for a loved one with Alzheimer's. The NIA publication *Alzheimer's Disease: Unraveling the Mystery*, lists the following:

The Negatives

Employment Complications: It's difficult to hold down a job and be responsible for the care of someone with Alzheimer's disease. Caregivers are often called away from work for various emergencies, and at times the ill person must be accompanied on visits to the doctor. The workday may also be interrupted by numerous calls from home. In addition, people frequently find that they are unable to concentrate on what they are doing when they are worried about what's going on at home. Ideally, caregivers shouldn't have other responsibilities to concern them, but not all caregivers are financially able to stop working and just tend to their loved ones.

Emotional Distress and Physical Fatigue: Caring for someone with Alzheimer's can be draining on many levels. Even when the caregiver is not actively working with the patient, that individual is always "on duty" to make sure that the person does not wander off or accidentally injure himself or herself.

Caregiving can also be physically exhausting. One woman found that she never got a good night's sleep while caring for her husband with Alzheimer's disease. This was partly because several times each night he'd wake up and think it was morning. He'd begin to get dressed and prepare breakfast. Even though he had been retired for years, sometimes he would even start to leave the house to go to work. Each time this occurred, his wife would get up and convince him that it was still nighttime and he needed to go back to bed. After a few weeks of this she was completely exhausted.

Social Isolation: Many caregivers feel isolated and cut off from others while caring for someone with Alzheimer's disease. This is especially true if they've left their jobs to take on this task full time. These individuals often find that they miss the intellectual stimulation and interaction they enjoyed at their place of employment. Even caregivers who were not employed outside the home often feel cut off from the outside world. They find that they are unable to leave the ill person very often to see friends or pursue other activities they once enjoyed.

Family Conflict: Caregivers are often conflicted about their obligations. Many caregivers are daughters with their own children, and when more than one person needs help at the same time, conflicts can erupt within the family. When adult siblings share the role of caregiver, there may be arguments over how the work and financial assistance is split up.

The Positives
A New Sense of Purpose and Meaning in Life: Some people come to see caring for someone who can no longer care for himself or herself as one of the most humane and valuable tasks they've ever undertaken.

Fulfillment of a Lifelong Commitment to a Spouse: It is always difficult to lose a beloved spouse, so many people cherish even this strained time spent with them.

Staff members at assisted-living facilities work with patients to help them retain as many skills as possible for as long as possible.

An Opportunity to Give Back to a Parent: This can be a very rewarding experience for adult offspring who consider caregiving an opportunity to show their parents how grateful they are to them.

Renewal of Religious Faith: Often family members find religion to be a wonderful source of strength in dealing with this difficult disease.

Close Ties with People Through New Relationships or Stronger Existing Relationships: Some caregivers make wonderful new friends through support groups and other Alzheimer's disease–related organizations. Sometimes, they continue working with these groups even after their loved one has died.

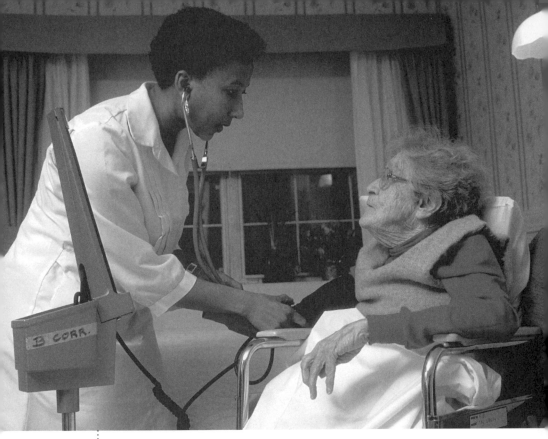

Residential care facilities can provide close supervision and ongoing medical care for patients with late-stage Alzheimer's disease.

LONG-TERM OUTSIDE CARE

As Alzheimer's disease progresses, the situation sometimes becomes too much for a caregiver to handle at home. Two types of residential care facilities are available for these cases. One is an assisted-living facility where people can get more care than may be available to them at home. At these facilities, residents are provided with meals, house-keeping services, and activities that they can still manage to do. These places will also take the residents to their doctors' appointments or for physical therapy sessions. If necessary, the staff at an assisted-living facility can help residents with bathing, getting dressed, and taking medications. Such facilities allow residents some independence while they are still able to handle it.

In the later stages of Alzheimer's disease, however, more intensive care is frequently needed. These patients often need help with eating and moving around. They may wander away unless closely supervised. Such individuals are often best off in a nursing home or skilled nursing facility. These places provide round-the-clock supervision, and some also offer physical and speech therapy.

The move to a long-term care facility often entails a period of adjustment for both the individual and the family. Regularly planned visits can help in these situations. In addition, a social worker is usually available to help the new resident and the family during the transition period.

Placing a loved one in a nursing home is an extremely difficult step even when it's the only reasonable alternative. It can be a heartbreaking decision and many people feel guilty about doing what they need to do. One woman was upset about putting her mother who had advanced Alzheimer's disease in a nursing home. She felt that she was abandoning a parent who had always been there for her. Fortunately, her own son was there to tell her how he felt about the situation. He said:

You are not casting her off, Mom. That is what you may think that you are doing. I wish there was some way I could help you understand how I see what is happening. You will never stop loving Nana. None of us will. And you do not love her less by moving her to a home. You are spending every minute of the day with Nana, and it is taking its toll. You must care for yourself as much as you care for her.[10]

This is a painful reality but one that many people who love someone with Alzheimer's disease must accept.

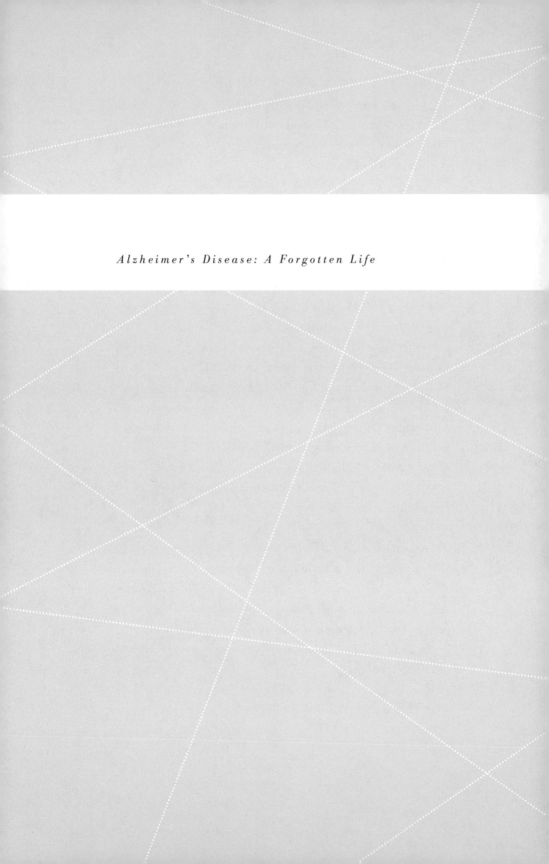

Alzheimer's Disease: A Forgotten Life

The Future 5

In Their Own Words: A Person with Alzheimer's Disease Speaks

Every time I have a feeling that I am losing—losing contact, losing my brains, whatever it is, I panic. I think the really worst thing is that you're so restricted, not so much by other people, but you just feel that you are half a person, and you so often feel that you are stupid for not remembering things or for not knowing things. . . . Nobody has restricted you necessarily, but the restrictions are very simple things of how far you can walk without getting lost, when you can do something. You always have the feeling it's pretty partial. And you always have the feeling, I know I do a lot of the time, that you just haven't done it right.[1]

The quote above is from Cary Smith Henderson who, earlier in his life, might have been viewed as a genuine American success story. Born and raised in the South, Henderson was the first person in his family to earn a college degree. But he didn't stop there. Henderson went on to get a Ph.D. in history from Duke University and eventually became a history professor at James Madison University. He was a brilliant teacher, a wonderful husband and father, and a man who appreciated his life. Then Henderson was diagnosed with Alzheimer's disease at age fifty-five, and he and his family painfully learned that nothing would ever be the same.

The slow diminishing of Cary Smith Henderson's mind is much more than a personal story. It's an everyday, real-life story for millions of Americans and their families who are trying their best to cope with the devastating effects of Alzheimer's disease. There are no happy endings. The best stories anyone can tell are those of people who, along with their loved ones, coped well after receiving a terrible diagnosis.

We need better stories, but we won't be hearing those until more is known about this disease and medical science comes up with better treatments or a way to prevent AD. Fortunately, in recent years, more research has been pointed in that direction, including a number of studies sponsored by the National Institutes of Health. Today more scientists than ever before are involved in Alzheimer's disease research. As Richard J. Hodes, M.D., director of the National Institute on Aging, testified before the Senate Committee Hearing on Alzheimer's Disease Research on April 1, 2003:

Fifteen years ago, we did not know any of the genes that cause AD, and we had only a limited understanding of the biological pathways that are involved in the development of brain pathology. Ten years ago, we could not model the disease in animals. Five years ago, we were not funding any prevention trials and had no ways of identifying persons at high risk for the disease. And as recently as two years ago, we did not understand anything about how AD's characteristic amyloid plaques and neurofibrillary tangles in the brain relate to each other.[2]

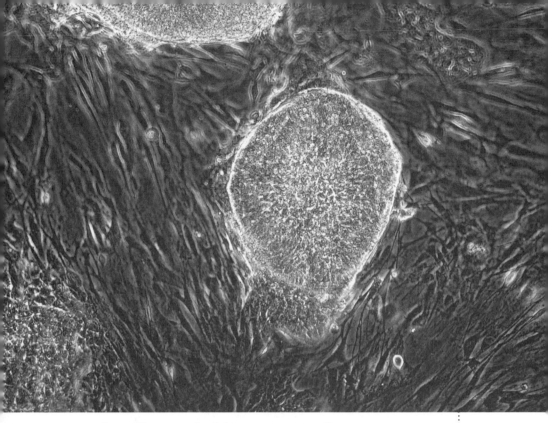

Stem cells may one day help treat or cure some diseases.

EMBRYONIC STEM CELL RESEARCH

One area that has received much attention is embryonic stem cell research. Scientists believe that these stem cells hold great promise for treating and possibly curing some diseases. These somewhat primitive cells have the ability to divide rapidly and produce more specialized cells, such as those found in brain and heart tissue. In Alzheimer's and other diseases in which a patient's brain cells are destroyed, the hope is that embryonic stem cells will be able to replace what's been lost by generating brand-new cells.

Embryonic stem cells also have potential for use in developing and testing new drugs for illnesses like Alzheimer's. If these cells can be used to create new brain tissue, researchers might be able to use this tissue to test new drug treatments before they are ready for use on animals and humans.

ASK DR. BROWNDYKE

Q: **What is functional MRI, and how is it used to learn more about the cognitive changes experienced in Alzheimer's disease?**

A: *Functional magnetic resonance imaging (fMRI) involves recording pictures of the brain that are ordinarily captured during MRI, in addition to collecting data about brain function over time. A person undergoing fMRI lies in a long cylindrical tube while the data are being collected. The patient is asked to perform some type of cognitive task, such as looking at pictures or remembering information. For instance, the person may wear goggles that display a screen on which words flash for a number of seconds. He may be asked to remember what the words were, and to respond by pressing a button with his finger when he sees a word he was shown before. This is one example of a type of recognition memory task that can be used in AD research.*

Data is collected for several groups of patients, such as a group of patients with early AD, another in the middle stages of AD, and a group of people without any memory deficits, known as the control group. Then it is analyzed to determine the differences in brain function between AD patients and the healthy control subjects. Pictures are generated to show which areas of the brain the healthy people in the control group use to perform tasks and where significant differences between AD patients and the control group exist. For instance, the brains of AD patients may demonstrate less activity in certain areas of the brain during memory tasks. This type of research allows us to better understand the cognitive decline associated with AD. The image on the next page shows an example of patients with AD compared with healthy control subjects. Note how the healthy controls show more activity than patients with AD in regions important to memory.

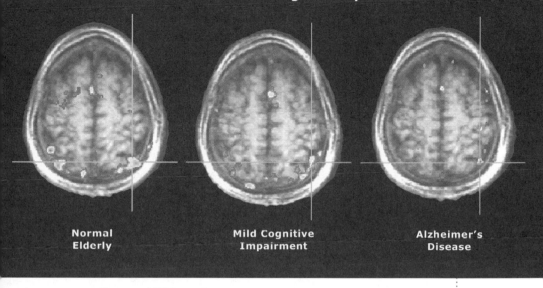

Functional Magnetic Resonance Imaging (fMRI) of Brain Activity Associated with Working Memory Abilities

Normal Elderly

Mild Cognitive Impairment

Alzheimer's Disease

Functional MRI provides images of how the brain functions during memory tasks and allows scientists to compare the brains of patients with Alzheimer's disease to those with normal memory function.

Through the years, however, there has been political controversy surrounding the use of embryonic stem cells in research. While embryonic stem cells may be highly desirable because of the tremendous variation in the types of cells they produce, many people feel that it's unethical to use these cells because they come from human embryos. They view embryos as developing human beings and believe that experimentation with them is morally wrong. A number of countries have banned this work, and the United States placed limits on federal funding for embryonic stem cell research in 2000.

Though groups in favor of embryonic stem cell research have been angered by the limitations placed on this work, some respected scientists have recently become more outspoken in their concern as to whether people with Alzheimer's disease would actually benefit from this research. It's been argued that Alzheimer's is not likely to be among the diseases that might someday be cured through embryonic stem cell treatment. This is because Alzheimer's disease is not a cellular disorder—it's a disease of the entire brain. People with Alzheimer's lose a tremendous number of different types of brain nerve cells, including countless connections or synapses.

"The complex architecture of the brain, the fact that it's a diffuse disease with neuronal [brain cell] loss in numerous places with synaptic loss, all this is a problem for any strategy involving cell replacement," noted Huntington Potter, a brain researcher at the University of South Florida in Tampa and chief executive of the Johnnie B. Byrd Institute for Alzheimer's Research.[3] These feelings were underscored by Michael Shelanski, codirector of the Taub Institute for Research on Alzheimer's Disease and Aging at Columbia University Medical Center in New York City, who stated: "I think the chance of doing repairs to Alzheimer's brains by putting in stem cells is small. I personally think we're going to get other therapies for Alzheimer's a lot sooner."[4]

So why do so many people believe that stem cell research holds great potential for people with AD? Perhaps Ronald D. G. McKay, a stem cell researcher at the National Institute of Neurological Disorders and Stroke, best summed it up when he said, "To start with, people need a fairy tale. Maybe that's unfair, but they need a story line that is relatively simple to understand."[5] Certainly his words are a disappointment to those who hoped a cure for Alzheimer's disease might result from stem cell research in the near future. Yet it's important

DRINK TEA AND SEE

Researchers at Britain's Newcastle University Medicinal Plant Research Center believe that drinking some types of tea may have an effect on the brain similar to that of some of the new medications for Alzheimer's disease. In a series of laboratory experiments, these scientists studied the properties of green tea, black tea, and coffee. While coffee had no significant effect, both types of tea were shown to reduce the activity of some kinds of enzymes related to the development of Alzheimer's. While no one thinks that these teas could be a cure for the disorder, it's thought that they might eventually be used as part of a treatment program to slow the course of the disease.

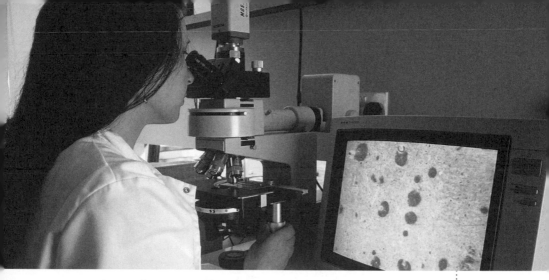

A researcher examines brain cells as part of a study on AD.

to remember that much of the research on AD is going on in other areas, and it is quite promising.

CLINICAL TRIALS

Researchers test new medications and strategies for dealing with a disease by conducting special tests or **clinical trials**. These take place in Alzheimer's disease research centers, medical centers, teaching hospitals, private research facilities, and doctors' offices. Sometimes these studies are quite costly and complex. They may be conducted over a number of years and can involve hundreds or even thousands of people. In some studies, the characteristics, lifestyles, and disease rates among different groups of people are compared. In others, a single group of people is observed over an extended period of time.

The National Institute on Aging is currently involved in two long-term studies to find out more about Alzheimer's disease. Both studies involve members of religious communities. One project, known as The Nun Study, dates back to 1986, and the only participants are nuns. The second project, The Religious Orders Study, is newer and is made up of older nuns, priests, and monks from thirty different religious communities throughout the United States. Both studies involve investigating the physical and mental capabilities of the participants over an extended period of time.

The participants in these studies undergo a full battery of medical tests each year. They have also agreed to donate their brains to science following their deaths. This allows researchers to compare the individual's brain tissue with many years of medical data collected through tests and examinations. Those in the study are volunteers and view their participation as a valuable opportunity to help others. As one nun noted: "[The researchers] can have my brain. What good is it going to do me when I'm six feet under?"[6]

The studies have already yielded some important information. This came from a use-it-or-lose-it study in which participants from The Religious Order Study were subjects. Over seven hundred nuns and priests provided researchers with information about the amount of time they spent watching television, listening to the radio, reading newspapers and magazines, reading books, going to museums, and playing cards, checkers, and puzzle games. After four and one-half years of tracking these individuals, the scientists found that the risk of developing Alzheimer's disease was 47 percent lower in those who engaged in these activities most frequently. These findings have been supported by other studies. We now know that mentally stimulating activities provide some protection against developing Alzheimer's disease.

STILL MORE STUDIES

At this time the National Institute of Aging is supporting eighteen clinical trials investigating various aspects of Alzheimer's disease. Seven of these are large-scale studies that are being conducted with the hope of finding ways to prevent Alzheimer's in the future. Some of the NIA trials are actively testing the effects of anti-inflammatory drugs, antioxidants, and other agents to evaluate their possible effect on slowing down the disease's progress, delaying its onset, or preventing the disorder altogether. Other clinical trials are being conducted to test the effects of various medications on lessening some of the behavioral symptoms of Alzheimer's disease, such as aggressiveness and wandering.

ASK DR. BROWNDYKE

Q: Why did some nuns who participated in the research studies retain their mental abilities despite a genetic predisposition to Alzheimer's and changes in brain structure related to the disease?

A: *The researchers carefully note the past history and the current physical and mental abilities of each of the nuns participating in the study. After the death of a nun, her brain is examined for abnormalities associated with AD, including senile plaques and neurofibrillary tangles. Despite the presence of severe levels of brain abnormalities and a strong genetic marker for the development of AD, some nuns had normal memory and other mental abilities. How was this possible when many other people with a similar profile were not able to learn new information or even to speak?*

The researchers concluded that the brains of some people were more resistant to cognitive decline. What made their brains more resistant to change? Examination of their histories showed that they had higher levels of education than other nuns (e.g., master's degrees). Other studies have also indicated that education may be a protective factor. Another factor associated with resistance to decline was an absence of significant head trauma over the life span of the person. In addition, the nuns who retained their cognitive abilities were actively engaged in everyday activities such as reading, knitting, and socializing. Another finding was that nuns who were happy tended to be engaged in more activities; depressed nuns were less likely to engage in a beneficial level of activity.

Nuns who retained their abilities tended to be free of strokes and vitamin deficiencies. These findings suggested that having risk factors in addition to those associated with AD might overwhelm the brain and lead to more rapid decline. The nun studies highlight the need for regular exercise and obtaining appropriate treatment for medical conditions such as high blood pressure and diabetes.

IMMUNIZATION AGAINST ALZHEIMER'S DISEASE—DREAM OR POSSIBILITY?

One exciting prospect on the research horizon is the possibility of developing a vaccine against Alzheimer's disease. Today people are routinely vaccinated against such diseases as measles, smallpox, and polio, but could this really work with AD? When a person is vaccinated against a disease, that individual is injected with a weakened form of the disease-causing bacterium or virus. In response, his or her immune system creates antibodies to fight the disease. This prevents the vaccinated person from coming down with the illness.

To come up with an effective vaccine against Alzheimer's disease, scientists experimented with mice that had gradually developed in their brains the beta-amyloid plaques that are characteristic of the disorder. The scientists injected these mice with a vaccine made of beta-amyloid combined with a substance designed to awaken the immune system. The researchers were pleased to find that over time significantly less beta-amyloid developed in the rodents' brains. The immunized mice also performed better on memory tests.

The research community was extremely excited by these results, and in time human studies to test the vaccine began. When the results looked beneficial, a further study was undertaken in the fall of 2001. This time, however, things didn't go as well. For the vaccine to be effective, high doses were needed, and these caused inflammation and bleeding in some of the research subjects. The study was stopped, but researchers refused to give up on the possibility of developing an Alzheimer's disease vaccine. They just viewed this as a temporary setback.

In late October 2004, a possible way around the problem was identified. Researchers from the University of Illinois at Chicago announced their preliminary success with a new method of immunization against Alzheimer's disease.

ASK DR. BROWNDYKE

Q:
Do brain cells in older individuals continue to grow?

A:
For many years, once an individual was fully grown it was thought that the brain was stable and unable to develop any further. While it is true that young brains tend to be more "plastic" and recover from injury more easily than older brains, studies are showing that older individuals also have some growth of cells in the brain at the microscopic level. For instance, both young and old animals that lived in an environment with complex stimuli to play with had more growth of dendrites than animals with a relatively impoverished environment. Dendrites are treelike branches extending from neurons. Neurons include the cell body, dendrites, and an axon. The neurons allow one area of the brain to communicate with another, and the dendrites receive these messages. Anytime people are involved in activities, this leads to small changes in their brains, such as increased connections between brain areas.

In AD these dendrites begin to lose their branches and the ability to generate new connections. In normal adult brains there are types of cells called pyramidal cells, resembling a tree with an elaborate root system and many branches. In early AD, the branches begin to whither. As AD progresses to the latter stages, only the trunk of the "tree" may be retained. This reduction in dendritic branches leads to loss of the usual connections between areas of the brain. As more and more connections are lost, the individual may lose the ability to think and remember.

Aware of the problems others had encountered in earlier studies, these scientists came up with a way to avoid having to use the large doses of vaccine that had previously caused inflammation and bleeding. Instead, they delivered a smaller dose of vaccine directly into a narrow space between the two hemispheres of the brains of mice with Alzheimer's disease plaques. Since the vaccine didn't have to circulate through the rodents' bodies where it could be absorbed, a significantly smaller dose could be given.

The results were very promising. The density of beta-amyloid was reduced in the mice brains, and no side effects such as inflammation or bleeding occurred. Neelima Chauhan, research assistant professor at the University of Illinois's College of Medicine, is enthusiastic about the study and noted: "The results suggest that periodic administration of the antibodies directly into the brain might offer a safer method for treating Alzheimer's. The vaccine reduces the accumulation of amyloid proteins for at least four weeks, providing a window during which other treatments could be used to prevent the formation of new plaques."[7]

While there still aren't clear and definitive answers about how Alzheimer's disease can be stopped or cured, the future now looks considerably brighter for people with this illness and their families. As NIA director Richard J. Hodes summed up his testimony for the Senate Committee:

The goal of AD research is ultimately to identify the most effective strategies for preventing and treating AD in diverse populations. Recent research findings have provided an unprecedented base of knowledge upon which to design these strategies. . . . It is difficult to predict the pace of science or to know with certainty what the future will bring. However, the progress we have already made will help us speed the pace of discovery, unravel the mysteries of AD's pathology, and develop safe and effective preventions and treatments, to the benefit of older Americans.[8]

Source Notes

INTRODUCTION

1. "Forgetting: A Portrait of Alzheimer's Disease." (PBS) http://www.pbs.org/theforgetting/experience/index.html.

2. Evan Thomas and Eleanor Clift. "As the Shadows Fell," *Newsweek* (June 21, 2004), p. 33.

3. Don Singleton. "Reagan Says He Has Alzheimer's Disease," *New York Daily News* (November 6, 1994), p. 5.

4. Anne Brown Rodgers. *2003 Progress Report on Alzheimer's Disease: Research at NIH.* Bethesda, Maryland: National Institutes of Health, October 2004, p. 2.

CHAPTER 1

1. "Forgetting: A Portrait of Alzheimer's Disease."

2. Ibid.

3. Alzheimer's Association. "New Alzheimer's Association Report Predicts Disease Will Soar 600 Percent Among Hispanics by 2050." Press release, May 18, 2004.

4. National Institute on Aging. *Alzheimer's Disease Fact Sheet.* Bethesda, Maryland: National Institutes of Health, March 2004. NIH Publication # 03-3431.

5. Rodgers. *2003 Progress Report on Alzheimer's*, p. 12.

6. Ann Charney. "What's the Matter with Claude?" *Saturday Night* (May 1998), p. 47.

CHAPTER 2

1. Anne Brown Rodgers. *Alzheimer's Disease: Unraveling the Mystery.* Bethesda, Maryland: National Institutes of Health, December, 2002. NIH Publication No. 02-3782, p. 34.

2. Ibid., p. 36.

3. Donna Cohen and Carl Eisdorfer. *The Loss of Self: A Family Resource for the Care of Alzheimer's Disease and Related Disorders.* New York: W.W. Norton, 1986, p. 21.

4. Denise Grady. "Alzheimer's Disease Steals More Than Memory: Violent Behavior Common." *The New York Times,* November 2, 2004, p. F1.

CHAPTER 3

1. Aaron Alterra. *The Caregiver: A Life with Alzheimer's Disease.* South Royalton, Vermont: Steerforth Press, 1999, p. 8.

2. National Institutes of Health. "Researchers Identify Brain Protein That Halts Progression of Alzheimer's." NIH NEWS-press release, October 26, 2004.

3. Ibid.

4. Ibid.

5. Ibid.

6. Cohen and Eisdorfer, p. 58.

7. Kathleen Fackelmann, "Fishing for Answers to Alzheimer's," *USA/TODAY,* November 16, 2004. http://www.usatoday.com/news/health/ 2004-11-16-fish-alzheimers_x.htm.

8. Ibid.

9. Alzheimer's Association. "Many Americans Worry About Brain Health But Only Half Keep Their Brains Fit According to New Survey." Press release, November 16, 2004.

CHAPTER 4

1. Pat Jordan, "Murderer or Model Husband," *50 Plus,* August 1988, p. 76.

2. Ibid.

3. Ibid., p. 77.

4. J. Madeleine Nash, "When Love Is Exhausted," *Time,* April 6, 1992, p. 24.

5. Ibid.

6. Ibid.

7. Cohen and Eisdorfer, p. 24.

8. Alterra, pp. 127-8.

9. Rodgers. *Alzheimer's Disease; Unraveling the Mystery,* p. 52.

10. Cohen and Eisdorfer, p. 238.

CHAPTER 5

1. Cary Smith Henderson. *Partial View: An Alzheimer's Journal*. Dallas: Southern Methodist University Press, 1998, p. 19.

2. Hearing on Alzheimer's Disease Research Before the Senate Committee on Appropriations, Subcommittee on Labor, Health, and Human Services, Education and Related Agendas, April 1, 2003.

3. Rick Weiss. "Stem Cells an Unlikely Therapy for Alzheimer's." *The Washington Post*, June 10, 2004, p. A03.

4. Ibid.

5. Ibid.

6. Rodgers. *Alzheimer's Disease: Unraveling the Mystery*, p. 38.

7. Hearing on Alzheimer's Disease Research Before the Senate Committee.

8. Ibid.

Glossary

acetylcholine: A chemical messenger in the brain that is a factor in memory and learning

Alzheimer's disease (AD): A degenerative illness that results in extensive mental deterioration and diminishing control of bodily functions

antioxidants: Substances that may help lower a person's risk for developing disease

antipsychotic medications: Drugs sometimes given to people with Alzheimer's disease to prevent violent reactions, restlessness, and hallucinations

APOE 4: A form of APOE found in significant amounts in the brains of Alzheimer's disease patients

apolipoprotein E (APOE): A common protein that normally assists in transporting cholesterol in the blood

autopsy: An examination of a corpse to determine the cause of death

beta-amyloid: An abnormal protein found in the brains of Alzheimer's disease patients

beta-amyloid plaques: Extensive clusters of damaged nerve endings

chromosome: A threadlike structure in a cell that contains the material that makes up genes

clinical trials: Test situations through which researchers try new medications and strategies for dealing with a disease

dementia: A brain disorder that seriously interferes with a person's ability to carry out everyday tasks and activities. Alzheimer's disease is the most common form of dementia.

early-onset Alzheimer's disease: An uncommon form of Alzheimer's that affects people between thirty and sixty years of age

free radical: A molecule that can build up in the nerve cells of the brain, causing a loss of function

gene: Heredity factor through which traits are passed from parent to child

late-onset Alzheimer's disease: The type of Alzheimer's disease that occurs in the elderly

neurofibrillary tangles: Diseased nerve cells containing twisted fibers

neurons: Nerve cells in the brain

neurotransmitters: The chemical messengers through which nerve cells communicate

oxidative damage: Damage to the nerve cells of the brain that upsets the delicate machinery that controls the flow of substances in and out of the cells

psychotropic medications: Drugs used to alter emotions or problem behavior

tau: A protein that gathers in tangled filaments in the nerve cells of the brains of people with Alzheimer's disease

transthyretin: A protein in brain cells that may protect the cells from the deterioration caused by Alzheimer's disease

To Find Out More

BOOKS

Altman, Linda Jacobs. *Alzheimer's Disease*. San Diego: Lucent Books, 2001.

Barmeier, Jim. *The Brain*. San Diego: Lucent Books, 1996.

Brynie, Faith Hickman. *101 Questions Your Brain Has Asked About Itself but Couldn't Answer . . . Until Now*. Brookfield, CT: Millbrook Press, 1998.

Hinnefeld, Joyce. *Everything You Need to Know When Someone You Love Has Alzheimer's Disease*. New York: Rosen, 1995.

LeVert, Suzanne. *The Brain*. New York: Benchmark Books, 2002.

McGuigan, Jim. *Alzheimer's Disease*. Chicago: Heinemann Library, 2004.

Walker, Richard. *Inner Workings of the Gray Matter*. New York: Dorling Kindersley, 2002.

Wilkinson, Beth. *Coping When a Grandparent Has Alzheimer's Disease*. New York: Rosen, 1995.

Willett, Edward. *Alzheimer's Disease*. Berkeley Heights, NJ: Enslow Publishers, 2002.

ORGANIZATIONS AND WEB SITES

Alzheimer's Association
225 N. Michigan Avenue, Floor 17
Chicago, IL 60601
http://www.alz.org

Alzheimer's Disease Education and Referral Center (ADEAR)
P.O. Box 8250
Silver Spring, MD 20907
1-800-438-4380
http://www.alzheimers.org

National Institute on Aging
Information Center
P.O. Box 8057
Gaithersburg, MD 20898-8057
http://www.nia.nih.gov/

Index

"2004 Maintain Your Brain Campaign," 68

Abandonment, 74–76
abstract thought, 15, 44
acetylcholine, 34, 56
Adkins, Shannon, 66
adult day care services, 84
African-Americans, 19–20
age, 9, 11, 18, 22, 33, 36, 61
aluminum, 42
Alzheimer, Alois, 16, 34
Alzheimer's Association, 18, 20, 68, 81
Alzheimer's disease
  causes of, 34–42
  characteristics of, 5, 14–16, 18, 22, 32, 44, 47
  conditions mistaken for, 22, 25, 27, 31-32, 36
  cure for, 12, 96
  stages of, 42–43, *43*, 45–49, *47*
Alzheimer's Disease: Unraveling the Mystery, 37–38, 85
Alzheimer's month, 69
amyloid proteins, 92, 102
antidepressants, 58–59
antioxidants, 63, 64, 66, 68
antipsychotic medications, 58, 60
apolipoprotein E (APOE), 35–37
apoptosis, 59
apraxia, 75
Aricept (donepezil), 56
Asian population, 20, 42
Ask Dr. Browndyke, 9-10
  apraxia, 75

atherosclerosis, 65
  brain cell growth, 101
  brain scans, 26
  cerebral atrophy, 33
  cognitive function loss, 50
  cognitive symptom testing, 44
  delusions, 60
  disease diagnosis, 13, 22
  driving with Alzheimer's, 78
  excessive glutamate, 59
  functional magnetic resonance imaging (fMRI), 94
  hallucinations, 60
  sundowning, 82
  The Nun Study, 99
assisted-living facilities, *87*, 88, *88*
atherosclerosis, 65
auditory hallucinations, 60

Baby boomers, 9
behavioral changes, 18, 45-48, 51–53, 58, 61
beta-amyloid protein, 32, 38–39, *39*, 40, 41, 62, 100, 102
blood pressure, 20–21, 40, 65, 68, 99
boxer's syndrome, 21
brain atrophy, 33, *33*
brain scans, 13, 24, 26, *27*, 33, *33, 50*
brain size, 32
Browndyke, Jeffrey, 9–10, 13, 22, 26, *33*, 44, 50, 59, 60, 65, 75, 78, 94, 99, 101

Cardiovascular system, 39–40
caregivers, 10, 23-24, 51, 52–53, *52*, 71, 76–77, *76*, 79–81, *79*, 80–81, 83–89, *87*, 89
Cassel, Christine, 74
cause of death, 12, 48
Center for Neurodegenerative Disease, 21
cerebral atrophy, 33, *33*
cerebral cortex, *32*, 62
cerebral spinal fluid, 13, 24
Chauhan, Neelima, 102
chemotherapy, 27–28
Cherokee Indians, 20
cholesterol, 20–21, 36, 40, 64, 65, 68
cholinesterase inhibitors, 56, 57, 58
chromosomes, 35, 38
clinical trials, 97–98
Coeur d'Alene Greyhound Park, 74, 75
Cognex (tacrine), 56
Columbia University Medical Center, 96
computerized tomography (CT), 26, 33, 65
coping techniques, *12*, 29, 58, 76, 80, 84
Cree Indians, 20

Davis, Patti, 7
delusions, 7, 51, 53, 60
dementia, 11, 21, 22, 23, 36, 44, 50, 60, 68, 69, 82
dendrites, 101
diagnosing, 13, 16, 22, 23–29, *24*
diet, 21, 40, 63–64, *64*, 66–67
disorientation, 14, 15–16, 72, 82
donepezil, 56
Down's syndrome, 23
driving, 16, 17, 66, 78, 83
drug reactions, 25, 27
Duke University, 9–10, 91
Duke University Medical Center, 9–10
dyspraxia, 75

Early-onset Alzheimer's disease, 18, 22, 35, 36, 62
education, 80–81

embryonic stem cell research, 93, *93*, 95–97
entorhinal cortex, 50
environment, 20, 42, 101
ethnicity, 19–20, 42
Exelon (rivastigmine), 56

Family history, 19
financial costs, 9
forgetfulness, 11, 14–15, 43, 46
Frangione, Blas, 36–37
free radicals, 41
Fritzsche, Harlan, 75
functional magnetic resonance imaging (fMRI), 94, *95*

Galantamine, 56
gender, 19
genes, 35–38, 62
Gilbert, Emily, 71–73
Gilbert, Roswell "Ross," 71–73
Glushak, Cai, 74
glutamate, 57, 59
Gulliver's Travels (Jonathan Swift), 15

Hallucinations, 47, 51, 58, 60
head injuries, 21, 25, 68, 75, 99
Head Injury Center, 21
heart disease, 20-21, 39–40, 65, 68
Henderson, Cary Smith, 91–92
high blood pressure, 20, 40, 65, 68, 99
hippocampus, 50, 59
Hodes, Richard J., 92, 102
Honolulu-Asia Aging Study, 42
hormone replacement therapy, 23

Immunization, 100, 102
inflammation, 41–42, 98, 100, 102

Jacques Cartier Bridge, 30
James Madison University, 92
Johnnie B. Byrd Institute for Alzheimer's Research, 96
Johnson, Jeff, 62
Joseph and Kathleen Bryan Alzheimer's Disease Research Center, 10
judgment, 7, 16

Jutra, Claude, 29–30

King Lear (William Shakespeare), 34
Kingery, John, 74, 75

Language problems, 45, 50
late-onset Alzheimer's disease, 35-38
Latino population, 20
life expectancy, 9, 12, 20
long-term care facilities, 89
loss of income, 36
lumbar punctures, 13

Magnetic resonance aniography (MRA), 26
magnetic resonance imaging (MRI), 26, 33, 33, 65, 94
mathematics, 15
Mayo Clinic, 6
McConnell, Stephen, 20
McIntosh, Tracey, 21
McKay, Ronald D. G., 96
medication, 56–59, 57, 60, 61, 97-98
memantine, 57–58, 59
memory loss, 13, 16, 22, 25, 27, 29–30, 31–32, 34, 43, 48, 50, 62
mental activity, 21, 67–69
metabolism, 27
mild cognitive impairment, 50
Mini-Mental Status Exam (MMSE), 44, 45
mood swings, 18, 22, 45, 51-53, 58-59, 84

Namenda (memantine), 57–58, 59
National Cancer Institute, 27–28
National Institute on Aging (NIA), 14, 23, 28, 41, 76, 84, 85, 92, 97, 98
National Institute on Neurological Disorders and Stroke, 96
National Institutes of Health, 37, 61, 92
Native Americans, 20
neurofibrillary tangles, 32, 50, 59, 65, 92, 99
neurological tests, 25

neurons, 32, 33, 38, 39, 40, 41–42, 96, 101
neuropsychologists, 44
neurotransmitters, 34, 38, 59
New York University Medical Center, 36–37
Newcastle University Medicinal Plant Research Center, 96
Newsweek magazine, 7
The Nun Study, 97–98, 99
nursing homes. See long-term care facilities.
nutrition, 14, 25, 27, 63–64, 64, 66–67

Olfactory hallucinations, 60
omega-3 fatty acids, 66
online support groups, 84

Personality changes, 7, 18, 46, 51–53, 79
physical activity, 67–69, 67
physiological changes, 27, 31–32
population, 19–20
positron emission tomography (PET), 26, 27, 50
Potter, Huntington, 96
prevention, 38-39, 61-62, 63, 66–67, 68, 69, 92, 100
programmed cell death, 59
psychological tests, 25, 44
psychotropic medications, 58, 59, 61
pyramidal cells, 101

Reaction time, 17, 78
Reagan, Nancy, 6, 7
Reagan, Ronald, 5–7, 6, 8, 69
The Religious Orders Study, 97–98
Remenyl (galantamine), 56
research, 56, 61–62, 63, 92, 93, 95–97, 97–98, 100, 102
rivastigmine, 56
routines, 16, 61, 81, 81
Rush University, 66

"Sandwich generation," 77
Schaefer, Ernst, 67
Senate Committee Hearing on Alzheimer's Disease Research, 92, 102
senile plaques, 37, 50, 65, 99, 102
sense of smell, 28, 60

Shelanski, Michael, 96
single photon emission computed tomography (SPECT), 26
sleeplessness, 59, 68, 84
Sparks, Larry, 20–21
stroke, 13, 25, 26, 40, 59, 65, 75, 99
substance P, 38–39
sundowning, 82
support groups, 83–84, 87
Swift, Jonathan, 15
symptoms, 5, 12, 14-16, 22, 32, 44, 47
synapses, 96

Tacrine, 56
tactile hallucinations, 60
tau protein, 39
Taub Institute for Research on Alzheimer's Disease and Aging, 96
tea, 96
testing, 8, 13, 22, 23- 25, 26, 75, 78, 100
Thomas, James, 46
transthyretin, 61–62

Tufts University, 66

University of California (Los Angeles), 66
University of Illinois at Chicago, 100, 102
University of Illinois College of Medicine, 102
University of Kentucky Medical Center, 20
University of South Florida (Tampa), 96
University of Washington (Seattle), 39–40
University of Wisconsin School of Pharmacy, 62

Ventricles, 50
visual hallucinations, 60
Vitamin C, 63
Vitamin E, 63
vocabulary, 15

Wandering, 12, 48, 49, 59, 82, 85, 89, 98

ABOUT THE AUTHOR

Award-winning author Elaine Landau worked as a newspaper reporter, a children's book editor, and a youth services librarian before becoming a full-time writer. She has written more than two hundred and fifty books for children and young adults. Among these have been texts on Tourette's Syndrome, Parkinson's disease, Lyme disease, cancer, tuberculosis, schizophrenia, head injuries, spinal cord injuries, blindness, and epilepsy.

Ms. Landau has a bachelor's degree in English and journalism from New York University and a master's degree in library and information science from Pratt Institute. She lives in Miami, Florida, with her husband and son.